THE CALL TO CLIMB

JAMES ROBBINS

THE CALL TO CLIMB

A STORY TO FIND YOUR PATH, CONQUER YOUR FEARS, AND FULFILL YOUR ■ DESTINY ■

WILEY

Copyright © 2025 by John Wiley & Sons, Inc. All rights reserved, including rights for text and data mining and training of artificial technologies or similar technologies.

Published by John Wiley & Sons, Inc., Hoboken, New Jersey.
Published simultaneously in Canada.

No part of this publication may be reproduced, stored in a retrieval system, or transmitted in any form or by any means, electronic, mechanical, photocopying, recording, scanning, or otherwise, except as permitted under Section 107 or 108 of the 1976 United States Copyright Act, without either the prior written permission of the Publisher, or authorization through payment of the appropriate per-copy fee to the Copyright Clearance Center, Inc., 222 Rosewood Drive, Danvers, MA 01923, (978) 750-8400, fax (978) 750-4470, or on the web at www.copyright.com. Requests to the Publisher for permission should be addressed to the Permissions Department, John Wiley & Sons, Inc., 111 River Street, Hoboken, NJ 07030, (201) 748-6011, fax (201) 748-6008, or online at http://www.wiley.com/go/permission.

The manufacturer's authorized representative according to the EU General Product Safety Regulation is Wiley-VCH GmbH, Boschstr. 12, 69469 Weinheim, Germany, e-mail: Product_Safety@wiley.com.

Trademarks: Wiley and the Wiley logo are trademarks or registered trademarks of John Wiley & Sons, Inc. and/or its affiliates in the United States and other countries and may not be used without written permission. All other trademarks are the property of their respective owners. John Wiley & Sons, Inc. is not associated with any product or vendor mentioned in this book.

Limit of Liability/Disclaimer of Warranty: While the publisher and author have used their best efforts in preparing this book, they make no representations or warranties with respect to the accuracy or completeness of the contents of this book and specifically disclaim any implied warranties of merchantability or fitness for a particular purpose. No warranty may be created or extended by sales representatives or written sales materials. The advice and strategies contained herein may not be suitable for your situation. You should consult with a professional where appropriate. Further, readers should be aware that websites listed in this work may have changed or disappeared between when this work was written and when it is read. Neither the publisher nor authors shall be liable for any loss of profit or any other commercial damages, including but not limited to special, incidental, consequential, or other damages.

For general information on our other products and services or for technical support, please contact our Customer Care Department within the United States at (800) 762-2974, outside the United States at (317) 572-3993 or fax (317) 572-4002.

Wiley also publishes its books in a variety of electronic formats. Some content that appears in print may not be available in electronic formats. For more information about Wiley products, visit our web site at www.wiley.com.

Library of Congress Cataloging-in-Publication Data is Available:

ISBN 9781394318421 (Cloth)
ISBN 9781394318438 (ePub)
ISBN 9781394318445 (ePDF)

Cover Design: Wiley
Cover Images: © enera/stock.adobe.com,
© Brandon Laufenberg/Getty Images
Author Photo: © James Robbins 2025

SKY10119046_061825

To Amber, Braden, and Sydney

My climbing partners for life

Contents

Warning		*ix*
SECTION I	**THE SUMMONS OF THE SOUL**	**1**
1	**Lost**	**3**
2	**Into the Night**	**11**
3	**The Storm**	**17**
4	**The Road to Nowhere**	**29**
5	**Cemetery of Souls**	**37**
SECTION II	**HONOR YOUR PATH**	**49**
6	**Copy and Paste**	**51**
7	**Beneath the Ice**	**61**
8	**The Examined Life**	**71**
9	**The Gift**	**81**
10	**Oh Captain, My Captain**	**89**

SECTION III   HERE THERE BE DRAGONS 95

11   **The Avalanche** 97

12   **The Mosaic** 107

13   **Into the Lair** 117

14   **Dragon Slayer** 127

15   **The Abyss** 139

16   **The Reflecting Pool** 151

SECTION IV   THE BEAUTIFUL STATE 161

17   **Making the Weather** 163

18   **Your Rope Team** 171

19   **Whiteout** 181

20   **The Dungeon Master** 187

21   **Three Little Birds** 197

SECTION V   A MOUNTAIN TO CLIMB 201

22   **The Worthy Pursuit** 203

23   **One Thousand Steps** 213

24   **High Camp** 223

25   **Walker of the Peaks** 235

Acknowledgments 241

About the Author 245

Index 247

Warning

What you hold in your hands is more than a book—it's an invitation.

A summons from your Soul, calling you to a conversation that might be long overdue.

But only if you're ready.

So, if you feel a pull toward something greater—a desire to live a more authentic and purpose-filled life—then turn the page.

Just know this: once you do, there's no turning back.

Congratulations.
Let's climb!

For special resources during your climb, visit:
www.iwillclimb.com

Section I

The Summons of the Soul

"Who looks outside, dreams; who looks inside, awakes."

—*Carl Jung*

Chapter 1

Lost

Bolivia, elevation 11,237 feet

I was lost.

I should have reached the highway two hours ago, but here I was, bouncing down some abandoned road in the Bolivian foothills. The map on my phone was insisting this was the way, but each mile made it clearer I was heading deeper into nowhere. I hadn't seen another car—or a house for that matter—in a couple of hours, and with the sun sinking fast, it would soon be dark.

I gripped the steering wheel tighter. If I couldn't find my way out of here soon, I would miss my flight back home. Worse yet, I was running out of gas and the last thing I wanted to do was spend the night in my rental car, in the absolute middle of nowhere.

What a fitting way to cap off what might be the worst day of my career.

I'd been in Bolivia for two weeks, along with our team from work, negotiating a land-rights deal with a remote Aymaran village. Nestled in the foothills of the Andes Mountains, these people had carved out a simple life for themselves, untouched by the modern world beyond their valley. Our biggest challenge had been the altitude. The entire team suffered from splitting headaches and nausea when we first arrived, but after a week our bodies eventually acclimatized.

Our client—a giant energy conglomerate—had located a large natural gas pocket on the edge of their village, and we were sent to convince the elders to let our client extract the gas. Pressure was always high in these negotiations, with millions of dollars on the line. The hardest part was convincing an untrusting group of elders to accept the deal. We'd sell them on the dream of prosperity, then gloss over the potential damage to their land and culture. It wasn't personal, just business. And if we ran into resistance, there were always bribes. I never actually saw that happen, but some of the team confirmed my suspicion when they told me that Rick, our boss, had done it several times.

I'd only worked for Rick for about a year. He was talented, driven, and arrogant. While he wasn't the most fun to work for, at least he was clear. Do things his way and you get rewarded. Oppose him, or underperform, and your life was going to be hell.

When we did close deals, which was often, there was a nice cash bonus in it for the team. The money was great, but deep down I could feel this job chipping away at my soul. In my quiet moments, I didn't feel proud of what we were doing.

And that's what ultimately led me here, driving alone in this crappy little car, without a clue of where I was.

Earlier today we were in a dimly lit community hall for our final meeting with the village elders. Rick made his closing pitch, reminding them of how good this opportunity would be

The Call to Climb

for the village. That was the part that always turned my stomach. It was a half-truth at best. The translator passed on Rick's final words to the elders who were seated at the head table. Then the five of them pulled their chairs together in a small circle to make a final decision.

As I sat, waiting, I felt a pang of guilt in the pit of my stomach. It wasn't the first time, but I'd learned to ignore it. After all, this wasn't my company, I just work there. But today, for some reason, I couldn't shake it. It began to rise into my chest, climbing like a fire up a spindle, searching for a way out of my body. I wanted to say something, but it wasn't my place. *We're not telling them the whole truth!* I thought to myself. *This is wrong!*

It was a fact that some of our previous deals had caused great harm to villages just like this one. The team pretended it never happened, but it had. "How can I sit here and be okay with this?" I asked myself. As the elders continued their discussion, time was running out.

I tried to swallow it, to ride out the emotion. "It's not my problem," I said to myself. But my conscience, now pounding on the door of my heart like an angry ogre, wasn't letting it go. I felt ashamed as it laid bare my cowardice. "Speak!" it cried.

I can't …

Then, without thinking, I blurted out, "There's one thing you need to know before you sign." The elders turned, surprised by my interruption. "This deal will make you a lot of money, but it can also do your village harm. I'm not saying it isn't the right move, but don't underestimate the impact to your way of life." I sat back in my chair, my breath shallow.

5

Lost

You could have heard a pin drop as all eyes were locked on me.

The elders then looked at the translator, who was still staring at me in disbelief. Out of the corner of my eye I saw Rick, his fist clenched around the tablecloth. It felt like time itself had stopped, and I immediately regretted what I'd done.

The translator turned and passed my message on to the elders. They returned to their huddle, speaking quieter now. Wanting to avoid eye contact with my team, I glanced down at my notebook and noticed my hand was trembling. I'd just detonated the deal, and probably my job along with it.

After what seemed like an eternity, the elders stopped talking. Then one of them stood up, walked over to Rick, and extended his hand with a big smile. "Vamos!" he said.

The team let out an audible sigh. Rick leapt to his feet and shook hands with all the elders. I was shocked but relieved I hadn't ruined everything.

After some paperwork and a group photo, we said goodbye to the elders and then headed outside. Rick's mood visibly changed as he marched past our SUV and to the compact rental car—the one nobody wanted to drive.

"*Riley!*" he yelled before getting in the passenger side.

I swallowed and walked toward the car. The team watched as I grabbed the door handle, braced myself, and got in.

Rick was six-foot-five, and inside the tiny car he seemed like a giant—an angry one. His face was hot, and a vein on his forehead pulsed with rage.

"*What the hell was that?*" he spat. "Millions of dollars on the line and you almost blew it with your moral bullshit!"

Rick clenched both his fists and for a moment I was afraid he might hit me. "You almost screwed over the whole team!" he fumed. "Was that your plan?"

"No," I said, my voice barely audible.

"If you're so goddamn concerned about the plight of the villagers, then maybe you should work for a charity. We just did them a favor Riley ... a *favor!*" Rick yelled.

He looked away and took a deep breath, trying to calm himself down. "I don't even want to talk to you for the rest of the trip, and when we get home, we're going to sit down and have a chat. You better believe it."

I didn't say a word. There was nothing I *could* say.

"Until then," Rick continued, "you can drive this junker back to the airport by yourself. The rest of the team will ride with me. It'll give you some time to think about what you really want to do with your life."

Rick got out and slammed the door behind him. The rest of the team followed as they clambered like puppies into the SUV. A moment later, they sped off, leaving me in a cloud of reddish dust.

That was six hours earlier. Now I was here, lost in the Bolivian wilderness. My phone was telling me to keep going, but the weird thing was I no longer had service. I couldn't even text the team. And I couldn't shake the feeling that I was heading farther from civilization rather than back to it. I bit my lip and scanned the horizon. Mile after mile of sand, rocks, and sagebrush reminded me I was a long way from home. Jagged, unforgiving hills rose on either side, and it looked like this place hadn't seen rain in months. My car was coated in dust—inside and out. It clung to everything, like regret, refusing to be shaken off.

I took a deep breath and focused my eyes on the road, but my thoughts kept returning to the meeting in the hall. As I replayed what happened, I heard a voice inside me. "What are you doing with your life, Riley?"

But I shook it away. Not now.

The sun finally disappeared behind the hills, taking with it the last rays of comfort. As darkness descended, the temperature plummeted fast, so I turned on the heater. *At least something works,* I thought. The road had now deteriorated so much that I had to slow the car to a crawl. Even then, the potholes and rocks that littered the road were unavoidable.

I didn't want to admit it, but I was scared. Scared of a lot of things. My job, my future, the team hating me, and the obvious: what might be waiting for me out there in the dark. Even the headlights of my car seem powerless to fend off the night.

Suddenly, out of nowhere, a violent crack sounded from underneath, as the nose of the car slammed into the earth. The impact made me bite my tongue.

"No, no, no …"

It felt like I'd just driven into a large hole, with the car's nose now pointed down on an angle. Confused, I stepped out into the night. The frigid air attacked my face as I walked to the front of the car. The flashlight beam danced across the dirt as I lowered myself to my knees. There was only a six-inch gap between the bumper and the road, but it was enough to have a look. Pressing one cheek onto the frozen dirt, I peered under the car, and when I saw it my stomach dropped. The axle had snapped in two, leaving both wheels splayed out uselessly into the dirt. Any hope of making it back to the city tonight was now gone.

I felt the panic rise in my throat. *I'm stranded. This day can't get any worse.* I calmed myself down with a couple of long, slow breaths to help me think clearly. I remembered a documentary I saw a few years ago on survival situations. They said it's always safer to stay in your vehicle and wait for rescue. *But what if the next village is just around the corner? I should at least check. But ...* I hesitated. *I don't know if that's a good idea.* I returned to the car to warm up and think.

The map!

I opened my phone again to discover my battery was now at three percent. I had let Jenny borrow my charger earlier today and she took it with her when they left. Not much time. I needed to hurry. I checked the map again, surprised to see the tiny blue dot still pulsing on the screen, marking my location. I collapsed it with two fingers, causing the map to zoom out. But there was nothing. I did it again, zooming out farther. Still nothing. Once more, I zoomed out, and at the very top right of the screen it looked like a couple of straight lines, like streets of a village. I tried to zoom out again....

Suddenly, the screen went black.

"Damn it!" I yelled in frustration.

At the same time, there was a flicker of hope. I only saw it for a second, but I'm sure it was a village, and it couldn't have been more than five miles away.

Lost

The question was, do I stay here, or do I go for it?

"It's pitch black out and freezing cold, and you have no idea where you're going," said a voice inside my head. "It's too risky. Just stay."

But this car felt like a coffin, and I didn't have enough gas to run the heater much longer. Then I felt something stir inside my chest—a voice, quiet yet urgent: *Move Riley. You've got to move!*

I sat a moment longer, my breath now fogging up the windshield. "Five miles?" I asked myself. "What the hell. Let's do it."

I reached into the back seat to grab my jacket. There was a village out there somewhere, I just knew it, and I was going to find it.

Chapter 2

Into the Night

Elevation 11,301 feet

Walking alone through the wilderness in a foreign country at night was terrifying. The overcast sky swallowed any hint of starlight, leaving me in near-total darkness. The icy air bit at my exposed skin, forcing me to switch the pocket flashlight between hands—one hand clutching it tightly, the other retreating into the shallow warmth of my pocket, desperate for relief.

But the most unnerving part wasn't the frigid cold or the darkness—it was the silence. The high-altitude desert doesn't come alive at night with a chorus of insects like back home. The only sounds were my labored breathing and the crunch of my shoes on the dirt. It felt haunting.

Every few minutes, I stopped to hold my breath while my ears strained the darkness for even the slightest sound. But there was nothing; not even a breeze to distract me from my thoughts. I don't think I've ever felt more alone. As I walked, I reflected back on the meeting earlier today. I definitely let my team down. I thought I was doing the right thing but I almost cost us the deal, which would have wiped out everyone's bonus. I felt so conflicted.

Thirty minutes into my journey, I started to have second thoughts. Was that really a village I saw on my phone? Every mile I walked down this road was one mile farther from the safety of the car. *I'm going to end up like one of those people in the documentary who leave their vehicle and wind up dead*, I thought. *Don't they have wild dogs out here?*

"Just keep walking, Riley," I told myself.

After about an hour, I began to shiver. The pain in my hand as I held the flashlight was unbearable, so I turned it off and put it back in my pocket. With nothing to light my way, I had to stop. It was pitch black. A growing panic welled up in my chest as I seriously questioned if I should turn back. In my pocket, my hand gripped the smooth stone I'd been carrying every day for over three years. My thumb ran across the numbers that were engraved onto its surface. It calmed me while I considered my options.

Slowly, my eyes adjusted and the faint outline of foothills off to my right faded into view. Apart from that, there was nothing but a dark, vast, empty space.

"What have you done, Riley?" I said out loud to no one.

And then, in the distance, I saw it—a light. It was barely perceptible, a tiny pinprick in the emptiness. Had my flashlight been on, I would have missed it.

My heart jumped. "I knew it." For the first time today, I felt a flicker of hope. With renewed energy, I picked up the pace and headed toward the light.

As I got closer, a second light appeared, and then a third. They were scattered across the ground like stars that had fallen to earth. A village!

I wasn't alone after all.

Then, a flash of lightning danced across the horizon, above the clouds, briefly lighting up the desert. It was followed by a low rumble of thunder off in the distance. *I didn't think you could have lightning when it's this cold, but if there's a storm coming, I don't want to be stuck out here.*

Thirty minutes later, the village began to take shape, as dark outlines of rooftops appeared on the horizon. A dog started barking, aware of my approach, and was quickly joined by another. This led to at least one more light coming on.

As I walked to the edge of the village, the light I'd first seen from a mile away now came into full view. It was a single bulb attached to a wooden pole with a small solar panel. As I got closer, I could see two men—one wearing a blue vest and leaning against the light pole, the other sitting on a chair next to the wall, wrapped up in a blanket.

I was relieved, but also cautious. I stopped, observing the men from a distance. Out here in the dark, I was invisible, and I wanted to know if they were safe to approach. Over my short time in Bolivia, I had passed through several small villages, and all of them had been friendly. But I'd never been alone, and never in the middle of the night.

The cold soon reminded me that I couldn't stay out here much longer. I had no choice but to go. Not wanting to startle them, I called out while still several yards away. "Hola," I said.

13

Into the Night

They turned, startled by the voice coming out of the dark. I slowly stepped into the light, raising my hands slightly to show that I was not a threat.

"Hola, hablas inglés?" I asked.

They both shook their heads. *That's not good*, I thought. *I don't speak Spanish, so this is going to be interesting.*

"My car-o is no bueno."

I cringed, my face apologetic for butchering their language. I fumbled for the words, but when they didn't come, I resorted to acting out what had happened with the car. It was history's most awkward game of midnight charades.

But they nodded their heads, which I interpreted as a good sign. Then they began talking excitedly to each other in Spanish before the man wrapped in the blanket said to me, "¿Está aquí para ver al Caminante de la Cumbre?"

I just stared at them blankly.

"I have no idea what you just said." I answered. Then it hit me that they had no idea I'd just told them I had no idea.

I searched my memory for the simple phrases I'd learned in high school. "No comprendo," I blurted out with a smile, proud of myself for remembering.

The man in the blue vest narrowed his eyes. "Okay, vamos," he said, and motioned for me to follow.

Keeping up with the two strangers wasn't easy. The streets were dark and uneven. Just when I thought I'd reached the safety of the village, I feared I was in danger once again. I had no idea where these guys were taking me. A few minutes later, they turned to the right and led me down a winding path, which cut between a row of houses. In here it was so dark I couldn't even see my feet. I hesitated for a moment, thinking maybe I should turn and run, but where? I was out of options.

We continued a few more feet and then stopped in front of a small house. Light flickered in a tiny window beside the door, allowing me to see some of my surroundings. The man in the blue vest went to knock on the door but pulled back his hand at the last moment, as if having second thoughts. I wondered if something was wrong, but more importantly, who lived behind the door?

The sky once more illuminated with lightning. The man in the blue vest looked at me and said, "El Caminante," then returned to the door. He took a deep breath, stood up straight, then carefully reached out his hand.

Knock, knock, knock.

15

Into the Night

Chapter 3

The Storm

Elevation 11,389 feet

The door of the small house creaked open, spilling light into the street. Because I was standing to the side, I couldn't see who stood in the doorway. The man in the blue vest began to speak. Respect has a distinct signature, and whoever he was talking to was someone held in high regard. I waited, feeling guilty for the late-night intrusion. Then the man in the house leaned out into the street, holding up a lantern in my direction.

He looked to be in his late fifties. His hair fell from his head in long, dark wavy locks interrupted by streaks of silver. His face was weathered, and the deep lines around his eyes suggested a lifetime of smiling. He looked at me, his eyes kind, and in his gaze, there was something else—recognition.

"Slightly off course, are we?" he said, his voice rich with a slight accent but in perfect English. "Welcome to our village, friend. You must be freezing. Come in, come in."

I let out a breath I hadn't realized I was holding. "Thank you," I said.

I entered the house, then turned back to my two guides still at the door. "Muchas gracias," I said.

They both chuckled and nodded, then disappeared into the night. The man closed the door behind me and said, "A storm is coming. You can smell it. You arrived just in time."

"I saw lightning on my way here," I said.

He set the lantern down on a small wooden table. "I'm Santiago. It sounds like you've had quite the day."

"You could say that again," I replied, unzipping my jacket, which was stiff from the cold. "I'm Riley," I added, extending my hand.

Santiago shook it firmly. His grip was warm and solid.

"Come. Have a seat by the fire and I'll make us some tea. You're obviously staying here tonight, unless you booked ahead at the Hilton down the road. They fill up fast."

"There's a Hilton hotel here?" I asked, eyebrows raised in surprise.

"No," he laughed. "But everyone always falls for that one. It never gets old."

He disappeared into the kitchen, still amused with himself. I'd only just met him, but I could sense there was a whimsical charm about him, an energy that immediately put me at ease. In any other circumstance, I'd have been on guard—alone, in a stranger's house, in a foreign country—but something about him made me relax.

I sank into one of the leather armchairs in front of the fire, its plump cushions hugging my cold and aching body. The smell of wood smoke mixed with a hint of kerosene brought back memories of visits to my grandfather's house when I was a child.

18

The Call to Climb

"Jorge and Carlos are on their way to retrieve your car," Santiago called from the kitchen. "They're the two who brought you here tonight."

"That's nice of them, but the axle is broken. So unless they have a tow truck, I don't think they'll have much luck."

Santiago returned carrying a tray with two small mugs of steaming tea. "Don't be too sure about that. They're quite resourceful. Besides, it looks like we're in for a long night, and they want to get it off the road. We don't get a lot of rain here, but when we do, it's like heaven itself empties out. It can be quite dangerous."

As if on cue, a rumble of thunder rolled overhead, much louder now.

Santiago handed me my tea. I wrapped both hands around the mug, hoping to get some heat into my fingers, which were still thawing. I took a sip. The fragrance was strong as the warm liquid slid down my throat. I hadn't realized how cold I was until now, sitting by the warmth of the fire.

"How did you learn English?" I asked.

"Oh, you know, a little here and there. I'm not as young as I look," he grinned. "And of course, all the visitors who stumble into Boca give me a chance to practice since I'm the only one in the village who can speak it."

"Boca?" I asked.

"Sorry, *Boca de las Cumbres*. That's the name of the village. It means 'Mouth of the Summits,' but people here just call it Boca. When you wake up in the morning, you'll see why. The village is at the base of some of the most beautiful peaks in the world. Everyone who visits Boca leaves changed—everyone."

19

The Storm

"I'm actually supposed to be on a flight right now back home, but you wouldn't believe my day."

I proceeded to tell Santiago everything that had happened, from our trip to Bolivia, Rick's meltdown after the meeting, and finally my frightening journey across the desert in the dark.

He listened intently and then said, "It never ceases to amaze me how people end up at my door."

"Others have come here?" I asked.

"Yes, of course," he answered. "The roads are not well marked, and when people try to use their phones for a map, well …" He looked at me slyly. "Let's just say that a lot of problems are avoided when you have the right map, Riley."

"Lesson learned," I chuckled.

"Your story reminds me of a man, not too long ago, who ended up here in the village. He was a talented executive, but he too had lost his way."

"Let me guess, phone map," I joked.

"Yes, but he was slightly off course in life as well. He'd devoted so many years to climbing the corporate ranks, only to realize one day that something was amiss. He couldn't understand it, because he was doing everything he thought he was supposed to do. But somewhere along the way, despite being handsomely rewarded, he'd lost his passion and felt a growing emptiness. It doesn't matter how much money you make, Riley—if you're out of alignment, it's not living at all."

"I can relate to part of that," I said. "I don't really like my job, especially after a day like today. It's weird—sometimes I feel like I'm in the wrong place, like there's something more for me to do. It's not a good feeling. But something's gotta pay the bills, right? So what happened to that guy?" I asked.

"He made a discovery that changed everything. He was able to finally bring his life into alignment with his soul."

"Wow, sounds like it was a great experience. Do you think there's such a thing as the soul, though?" I asked.

"Oh yes, Riley," he replied adamantly. "In fact, let me tell you something." He sat up in his chair and leaned forward. "Your soul has been with you since the day you were born. It's the deepest, most authentic part of you—your true self, the part that knows the real reason why you're here."

"That's the million-dollar question, isn't it?" I asked. "Why are we here?"

I hadn't told anyone, but this was the question I had been wrestling with for quite some time. My life had so many disappointments from things I'd tried and failed. Each one started with excitement, as if I'd stumbled on my purpose in life, only to have it go down in a ball of flames. I was beginning to think there was no such thing as purpose. Only survival.

"Your soul knows why you're here," he said. "But the problem, Riley, is that life can be a difficult journey for the soul. Its path is often filled with obstacles and detours. There are also powerful forces that oppose it—most of which come from within you."

"Hmm," I grunted. "Forces within us that oppose our soul? Why would we do that?" I asked.

"Because your soul's intent is to walk its own path, and this turns out to be risky business."

"How so?"

The Storm

"Because not everybody is going to approve of what your soul desires to do. In fact, living in service to your soul is often at odds with living in service to the herd. As was said long ago, 'No one can serve two masters.' But your soul is not concerned with the opinions of the herd. Unfortunately, other parts of you are."

Just then, I heard a small ping above my head. Then another. It was the sound of raindrops hitting the tin roof outside.

"Here it comes," said Santiago, as he looked up at the ceiling.

The rain turned from a few drops to an all-out downpour in less than a minute. The wind whistled and howled, announcing its arrival with violent gusts.

Santiago continued. "On a night just like this one, there was a woman who wandered into the village. She was a successful surgeon. By the time she'd turned thirty-five, she'd already accomplished most of her goals. But one night, while sitting in her car before walking into her house, it hit her. 'I hate my life,' she said out loud, and then felt immediately guilty for uttering the words. After all, she had more money than most of her friends and was respected in the community. But still, something wasn't right."

"That's too bad," I said. "Especially since she was so accomplished."

"Yes, but it's not uncommon. Have you ever had the feeling, perhaps while on a vacation or stuck in morning traffic, that something was not quite right, as if somehow the path you're on isn't what you're supposed to be doing?" he asked.

"Yeah," I laughed. "About three hours ago."

The truth was, I felt those things a lot. But I'd buried them under deadlines and obligations. Who has time to get reflective when you have bills to pay? I just didn't tell anyone.

"These moments are nudges from the soul," he said, "trying to get your attention because something is out of alignment."

"Out of alignment with what?"

"When people are younger, they don't think much about the soul. They're just trying to fit in, learn the ropes, and not get embarrassed. But as they mature into adults, the soul invites them to step into a larger agenda—an agenda that is often frightening. Because the soul is not driven to seek approval from the crowd, but rather to fulfill its destiny."

"Its destiny?"

"Yes, your soul seeks to bring into the world that for which it was created."

"So the surgeon hating her life—are you saying those were nudges from her soul?" I asked.

"Yes. Imagine you're driving a car down the road of life, but your soul knows a better path—one that's designed just for you. So it begins to pull the steering wheel slightly to one side. But instead of following it, you fight with the wheel and pull the car back in line."

"So is that what you mean by living your life out of alignment? That you're driving down one road, but the soul wants you to go down another?"

"Exactly. And because your soul's determined to fulfill its destiny, it presses its agenda even harder. If you don't listen to the gentle tugs on the steering wheel, it might eventually bring

23

The Storm

the entire car to a grinding halt. When the soul's nudges are ignored, it eventually withdraws its energy, creating symptoms you can't ignore—anxiety, depression, or even a crisis. But sadly, even then, most refuse to show up for the appointment with their soul."

I'd never heard anyone talk about the soul like this. I always paired the topic with religion. But what he said resonated with me. I had felt the nudges, the tugs on the wheel, but I didn't think I had the luxury to pursue my passion. Most days I was just trying to get everything done to avoid taking my work home with me. But for all of the activity, I felt like I was never getting ahead. Weekly, I could feel the pressure that I was running out of time.

"This was the situation with the surgeon," Santiago continued. "She was experiencing a collision of 'selves.' There was the self she had constructed in her earlier years, and then there was her soul. But each one was on a different path. The more messages the soul sent, the harder she worked to ignore them. Until eventually the summons was too loud to ignore, and that's what brought her here."

Just then, a flash of lightning lit up the entire house, followed immediately by an explosion of thunder that sounded as if it had ripped a hole in the sky itself. The house trembled.

Santiago looked at me with eyes opened wide. "That was close," he said.

"Are we going to be okay in here?" I asked.

Santiago looked up at the ceiling again. "I think so," he said, in an unconvincing way.

The Call to Climb

"So what happened to the surgeon?" I asked, trying to distract myself from the storm.

"She finally honored the appointment with her soul, and high up on the mountain she realized that much of her life had not been her own. Like a character in a play, living out a script she didn't write, she saw that many of her choices had been swayed by the values of others. And in her case, her parents' dreams had somehow become her dreams."

"This was on the mountain?" I asked slightly confused. "Was she a climber?"

"We're all born to climb, Riley. But there's a special mountain, not too far from here. Some even call it magical. It called her to climb so that she might finally attend the appointment with her soul."

With the fire dying, the room was almost dark. Santiago walked over to the small pile of wood stacked beside the fireplace. I could see his silhouette as he meticulously sorted through the logs like a carpenter trying to find the right piece for his project. Settling on one from the pile, he gently laid it on the dying flames. Tiny sparks burst from the ashes and scurried upwards into the chimney.

"The mountain called her?" I asked. "You sound like my grandmother. Every time she wants us to take her to the beach she tells us the ocean is calling."

"Your grandmother sounds lovely, but no, not like that."

Santiago sat back down in his chair and stared at me. His eyes were like deep pools that held secrets from long ago.

"Do you know why you're here, Riley?" he asked.

25

The Storm

The question surprised me and made me feel uncomfortable, as if I'd overstayed my welcome. "Well," I stammered, "I came to Bolivia with work, and then of course everything that happened today with the car."

Santiago gently shook his head as if I'd given the wrong answer.

"You're here because you too were called. In fact, we've been expecting you."

Lightning flashed again, this time like a strobe, as a crack of thunder exploded above.

I smiled nervously, hoping this was another of his playful jokes, but he just continued to stare, his face void of expression.

"I told you this mountain is a special place. It chooses people to come here and climb. They arrive from all over the world, stumbling their way into this tiny village, for a long overdue appointment with their soul." He paused to let me absorb what he was saying.

"And tonight, that person is you."

"Whoa," I laughed, trying to break the sudden tension. "I'm here because my car broke down, nothing more. This was definitely not on my itinerary, and I'm certainly not a climber," I protested.

"Yes, everyone says the same thing. 'I missed my turn and got lost.' 'I ran out of gas.' 'My car broke down on the road.' The stories are slightly different but they all end the same—knocking on my door, and sitting in the very seat where you are now."

I felt the hair stand up on the back of my neck and my arms exploded with goose bumps. A shiver went all the way down my spine. This guy is crazy. Part of me wanted to leave … but

26

The Call to Climb

I was trapped here. Yet something in his eyes, the quiet certainty, held me in place.

Santiago leaned in closer. "Do you think it's an accident that you're here?" he continued. "Your boss, the car, the desert, the storm," he pressed.

"Riley, your soul desires to have a conversation with you, but up to this point you have avoided the appointment, instead drowning out its invitation with the busyness of your life. So it has brought you here, to this barren place, in the hopes that the two of you at last might sit, and you, perhaps for the first time, will clearly hear its voice."

I swallowed hard, not sure how to respond. "What are you saying?" I asked.

"I'm saying that you've been called to climb. The question is, Riley, are you ready for a conversation with your soul?"

I looked out the window, feeling both conflicted and confused. Outside the sky roared with fury, as if the heavens themselves were tearing apart. I wondered if any of this could be true. Was my soul really calling me to climb some mountain? That sounds like the kind of thing you do when you have your life figured out, not when you're lost, tired, and barely hanging on. Could there be a different path out there, one that *was* more aligned with my soul? Part of me wanted it to be true, that there was something greater for my life. But the rest of me found all of this impossible to believe.

The Storm

Chapter 4

The Road to Nowhere

Elevation 11,389 feet

I don't know how long I slept, but when I woke up the sun was already streaming into the bedroom. At first, I didn't know where I was. But as sleep drained from my head, the events of yesterday came flooding back in. Rick's conversation was still fresh in my mind, and Santiago's talk about a mountain, and my soul … was that even real?

I quickly got dressed and went into the bathroom. Inside was a tiny mirror, barely big enough for me to see my face. A tired gaze stared back at me. My eyes had dark circles under them and I looked like hell. "What happened to you, Riley?" I whispered to myself. I walked out into the living room, but it was empty. The fire that was so pleasing last night was now a pile of ashes. The house was quiet, and the front door had been left open just a crack. I walked outside and was immediately blinded by the sunlight. Squinting, with one hand above my eyes, I stepped out of the house and onto the narrow street. I now saw the rough cobblestone path that I had stumbled down last night when I arrived.

As my eyes finally adjusted to the sun, I looked up and couldn't believe what I saw. Three towering peaks rose up from the earth and surrounded the entire village. They were massive—gigantic monsters of black rock, covered in snow and ice. Huge seracs hung high on ridges near the top. I'd never seen anything so spectacular. "Wow," I said. "Just wow!"

Last night's conversation with Santiago came rushing back to my mind. I realized that I had been overly emotional yesterday, overwhelmed by everything that had happened. It made me more vulnerable to all his talk about the soul. In the daylight, though, his words felt even more absurd. I wouldn't be climbing anything. I just needed to find my car and get back home, then see if I could still save my job.

I turned to head back into the house when I heard footsteps from behind me.

"Riley," said Santiago with a cheerful smile, "how did you sleep?"

"Fantastic," I said. "I was so tired that I crashed right away. I don't even know what time it is."

"Ha," laughed Santiago as he placed his hand on my shoulder. "Neither do I. I don't own a watch."

I looked up at the peaks above. "You were right. That is beyond words. When I arrived last night, I had no idea."

Santiago looked up and smiled. "They're called Las Tres Hermanas, the Three Sisters. People here believe they stand watch over the village." His eyes sparked with admiration. You could see he loved the mountains, and who could blame him?

"They're beautiful," I said. "And to think that last night you wanted me to climb one of those?" I laughed. "I can handle myself in the climbing gym, but this is a whole different world. I'd die up there."

Santiago turned back to me. "Oh not one of those, Riley. The mountain I spoke of is farther up the valley, and much bigger. If you think these mountains are amazing, wait until you see that one."

I don't know why I hesitated to break the news. I felt like I was letting him down, but I wasn't climbing any mystical mountain.

"So, here's the thing." I said delicately. "I'm not going to be able to climb your mountain, or any others for that matter. I just need to get home, or I might not have a job when I get there. But I want to thank you for your hospitality. If I had not found you, it would have been one uncomfortable night. Honestly, who knows if I'd have survived. It was an honor to meet you. But I really need to go. I'm sorry."

Santiago stared at me with the most compassionate eyes I'd ever seen, which made me feel worse.

"I just need to call the rental car agency and get them to come pick me up."

Santiago nodded his head. "I understand, Riley. I really do. I would never want you to do anything against your wishes."

"Thank you," I said, feeling relieved.

Santiago took a long deep breath. "I have some good news, and I have some bad news. Which would you like first?"

"I don't like the sound of that," I said. "Let's have the good news first, since yesterday was such a mess."

"The good news is that the guys were able to get your car last night and tow it back to the village."

31

The Road to Nowhere

"Wow, you were right about them. And that is good news because my suitcase is still in the backseat. Now what's the bad news?"

"It's the road." Santiago paused, which made my heart skip a beat. "There was a massive mudslide last night that buried it completely. Not only that, but farther down the valley, the bridge was washed out by a flash flood. It was a bad storm."

"Oh man, I'm sorry to hear that. Will that impact the village much?"

"No, we're used to this. Up here, the weather is the boss."

"Ok, well I'm assuming there's another way back to the airport. I just need a phone."

Santiago drew in his lips like a child about to make a confession.

"What is it?" I asked.

"The road. I'm afraid it's the only way in and out of the village. We are called Mouth of the Summits for a reason. We're all stuck here until they get it cleared."

"*What?* You gotta be kidding me!" I stared at him incredulously. "I can't stay here. I need to go." I felt a rush of panic. "What am I supposed to do?"

"I'm sorry, Riley," he said.

I paced back and forth on the narrow street trying to think of my options. But I had none.

"Can I walk out of here? Have someone meet me on the other side?"

"Even if you tried, you couldn't get across the river. It's too dangerous. Right now, the road back to civilization is a road to nowhere."

32

The Call to Climb

"How long until they open it?" I asked.

"The last time this happened it took five days. But last night's storm was even worse. The guys think it will be ten."

"*Ten days!?*" My voice echoed down the narrow street. I wanted to throw something, anything.

I sat down on a wooden crate that was beside the house. "I need a phone. I must call my work. Do phones even work here?" My voice was laced with irritation.

"I thought you might need one, so I brought this." Santiago put his hand on a small black case that hung by his side. I hadn't even noticed him carrying it.

"It's one of only two satellite phones in the village. But it's fully charged and ready to go."

He opened the case and handed me the oversized phone. We had rented one just like it when we arrived in Bolivia in case of an emergency.

I was going to call Rick, but his number was on my phone, which was dead. It hit me that I didn't know any of my team's phone numbers even though we texted each other all the time. Then I remembered I had Tony's business card in my wallet.

I quickly found it and dialed his number, but Tony didn't answer. I dialed again and let it ring. "C'mon Tony ... answer."

Finally on the sixth ring he picked up.

"Hello? ... Who's this?"

"Tony! It's me, Riley. Oh my goodness, I'm so glad you answered.

"Riley! Where are you? Are you okay? We've been worried sick."

"Yeah, I'm fine, but you won't believe where I am."

33

The Road to Nowhere

I explained the basic details he needed to know but left out my cryptic conversation with Santiago.

"Here's the thing," I continued. "I'm stuck in this village until they can clear the road. It could be up to a week."

"Bummer, man. I'm sorry," replied Tony. "I think you better talk to Rick. He's actually right here. One moment."

Before I could protest, Tony was gone.

A minute later, he returned.

"Riley? Rick wants to talk to you...."

I closed my eyes and took a long, deep breath, then braced myself.

"Riley," Rick's voice was calm but serious. "Tony told me what happened and we're glad you're okay. Listen, we need to have a conversation when you get back here. HR has instructed me that we can't do it over the phone, but I just wanted to give you a heads-up. We're also busy right now finalizing the logistics of the deal, so we don't really need you." Rick paused.

"If I were you, I'd find a way to enjoy your time while you're stuck in Bolivia. I gotta run."

With that, Rick hung up the phone. I didn't even get to say a word. Not a single word.

"Everything okay, Riley?" asked Santiago.

"I think—I just got fired. Well, not officially, but unofficially until I get back to the office, and then it'll be official."

Santiago didn't say anything. We both just stood there.

"Me and my big mouth," I said. "I should have just stuck with the plan. It's like they say, 'No kind deed goes unpunished.' Who did I think I was?"

34

The Call to Climb

The thought of being fired was another blow to my ego. After my business failed, I wanted something stable, and this job gave me that. But I had ruined it.

"I just want to go home," I said.

We walked back into the house, and I returned to the leather chair, feeling defeated. All the details from last night's conversation came rushing back into sharp focus.

Santiago sat down but didn't say anything at first. A moment later, he spoke. "Decisions ... do you know the origin of that word?"

I shook my head.

"It comes from the Latin word *decidere*, which means to cut off. By cutting off other options, you are left with only one path to focus your energy."

"Are you saying the storm was part of some bigger ... plan?" I asked sharply, tired of talking about mountains and souls.

"Not a plan, Riley," he said. "But a path."

Santiago leaned forward in his chair, his eyes holding mine. "A path that was meant for you. Can't you see what's happening?"

My anger ignited. It was like a fortress wall, protecting me from truths I didn't have the strength to face. Yet at the same time, I could feel it crumbling, brick by brick, leaving me vulnerable to the message trying to penetrate my heart. I wanted to fight, tell Santiago he was wrong, but deep down, something stirred.

Something that terrified me.

I felt my throat constrict and the world seemed to spin slightly as if everything I'd known was being pulled out from underneath me.

35

The Road to Nowhere

It was true. Something was out of alignment in my life. I'd felt it for a long time, and I was tired of struggling, tired of failing.

"I can't climb your mountain," I said, my voice shaking with emotion. "I don't even know where to begin."

"You don't have to know everything," said Santiago softly. "You only have to take the first step. The rest of the path ... will come."

I sat there, torn between two worlds—the life I'd always known, where things made sense, even if they didn't always feel right—and this place—the mountain and its call to something larger.

And deeper still—a part of me was begging for me to say yes.

I looked out the window where one of the jagged peaks could be seen. I felt a strange sense of awe mixed with fear. But beyond fear there was something else—something I hadn't felt in a long time.

Hope.

"What are you going to do, Riley?" he asked.

I knew deep inside I was standing at the fork of two paths. One of them was old and familiar, and the other—unknown, yet alluring, as if just beyond the bend lay something I was supposed to discover.

I took a long deep breath. "I'll climb," I whispered, almost to myself. Then louder, "I'm going to climb."

36

The Call to Climb

Chapter 5

Cemetery of Souls

Elevation 12,007feet

Santiago said the trek to base camp would take us five hours. Two young porters had already gone ahead of us to set up camp. I was grateful because my pack was heavy enough, filled with leftover gear and clothes from someone who had climbed before me.

Mile after mile we continued our slow ascent up the valley, which was flanked by the towering peaks we saw from the village. The landscape was both barren and beautiful, a kaleidoscope of black, gray, and white. We followed the river along the valley floor for over an hour. It was a captivating shade somewhere between turquoise and green as it flowed past us.

After a couple of hours, we veered away from the river and began climbing up to the right. The valley began to disappear beneath us as we gained altitude. "Up here, Riley. You're going to want to see this," said Santiago.

I followed the rocky path until I reached the crest of the hill. Then I looked up and saw it. A monstrous pyramid of rock, snow, and ice rising from the valley floor and high into the clouds. The summit itself seemed to scrape the sky. Jagged peaks erupted from pristine glaciers high on the mountain as giant seracs hung perilously from steep ridges. At any moment they looked like they could break loose and tumble down the mountain. The scene was breathtaking but also magnified my doubts. *There's no way,* I thought.

"I present to you La Montaña," said Santiago.

"Doesn't that mean 'The Mountain'?" I asked.

"Yes. It's the mountain with no name."

"Whoa, that's the most beautiful and yet terrifying thing I've ever seen," I said.

"That's a good way to put it," said Santiago, laughing. "It's easy to die up there if you don't know what you're doing."

"You do know what you're doing, right?" I asked. Santiago responded with a playful wink, which wasn't reassuring at all.

"How come I've never seen this mountain before in photos? Surely someone would have uploaded at least one by now."

"This is a sacred place, Riley. You won't find it on any map. In fact, the only way to see it is to be invited."

It was hard to look away. There were almost no words to describe it accurately.

"Speaking of invitations, I forgot to tell you. There's another climber joining us. His name is Osvaldo. He helps me on these adventures. He'll be arriving in camp later tonight, but for now, we need to pick up the pace. It'll be dark soon, and we still must make a quick stop."

About an hour later, Santiago veered off the main path and started climbing up a small hill. At the top was a large man-made cairn of rocks piled about six feet high. Attached to its

38

The Call to Climb

sides were a half dozen aluminum-looking plates. They were dented and weathered, but there were people's names etched in the metal.

"What are these?" I asked.

"Monuments," answered Santiago softly. "These are the names of those who perished on the mountain. Every time we climb, we stop here to remember them, to honor them."

"*Died?*" I asked.

I pulled my hand out of my pocket to touch one. It was cold and sent a shiver through my body.

"These were people like me, who were called to climb?" I asked.

"Yes," said Santiago somberly.

"But why would they die here if they were called?" I asked. "I would think they would be protected."

Santiago replied calmly, "This mountain is special, but it's also a dangerous place. You can't control everything that happens up there. But the same is true in life, Riley. Somewhere in the world today a person died on their way home from work. Do you think they ever considered that when they left the house this morning, it would be the last time they saw their loved ones?" Santiago paused. "Life cannot be tamed; it must be lived. This is why it's so sacred."

"I just thought ..." my words trailed off.

"You want to believe that because you accepted the call to climb, you're somehow shielded from harm. I understand— people do this all the time. They think if they live good lives, make all the right sacrifices, then nothing bad should happen to them. But when tragedy strikes, they're left asking, 'Why

39

Cemetery of Souls

would God let bad things happen to good people?' It's then they realize, with shock, that the karmic contract they've relied on for security was never signed by God. That's when they're faced with the truth: Life is far wilder and more unpredictable than they ever imagined. It shakes them because they've spent their entire lives trying to create a controlled and predictable world. But the soul, it craves something much larger."

The sudden reality that I could die on the mountain spiked the anxiety in my chest as I struggled to get a full breath.

"I don't know if I can do this," I whispered.

"Of course you can," Santiago answered. "Let's keep going."

As we drew closer to the base of the mountain, it seemed to stretch higher into the heavens. The wind picked up as biting cold air descended from the icefields above us. The brilliant blue sky I'd enjoyed all morning was being overtaken by dark clouds. Soon they enveloped the summit, making the mountain look even more ominous.

"Weather seems to be turning," I said. "I hope we're not in for another storm."

"It's okay," answered Santiago, unfazed by the sudden change. "This is your climb, Riley. The mountain acts as a sort of mirror. The closer we get to it, the more it reflects what's going on inside of you."

Santiago stopped and waited for me to catch up.

"Stormy in here," he pointed to my chest. "Stormy up there."

Normally I would have laughed at such a ludicrous suggestion, that somehow my inner life affected the weather, but the last twenty-four hours had taught me there are things about the universe I don't understand.

Up ahead, four tiny yellow tents and one larger green one came into view. They were the only specks of color in an otherwise washed-out wasteland.

"Hey, can I ask you a question?" I asked.

"Of course."

"At your house, you were talking about the soul and its desire for expression and meaning. But if that's a part of me that wants my attention and is seeking a conversation, then who am I in all of this?"

"Good question," said Santiago. "Yes, your soul embodies your higher self. It's like the seed of the oak tree, on a mission to become what it was destined to be. But there's another part of you, and that's the part that just asked me the question. You can think of it as your constructed self. Many call it the ego. It's the identity you've assembled over the course of your life based on your experiences, your beliefs, and your achievements, all of which you project to others."

"So the ego is the one driving the car down the road when the soul pulls on the steering wheel. Right?" I asked.

"Yes, correct. The ego isn't bad, it's just limited. While your soul seeks meaning, the ego seeks comfort and protection, often in the context of the herd. When the ego's in charge, you can easily veer off course because it's more concerned with surviving the moment than following a deeper purpose."

"I can see how those two might not always agree with each other," I said.

"No," Santiago said, and laughed.

We reached camp just before we had to turn on our headlamps. Juan and Luisa, our two young porters, greeted us

41

Cemetery of Souls

enthusiastically. One of them handed me a mug of tea and a small piece of chocolate. It was the best I'd ever tasted.

In the camp were four tents for sleeping and one large cook tent where you could actually sit at a small table. Inside was a stove that hissed in the dark as its blue flames battled the cold. On top sat a black pot with steam rising from one side of the lid. Whatever it was, it smelled delicious.

After stowing my things, I returned to the cook tent, where Santiago was dishing up two bowls of quinoa soup. I relished every sip as I tried not to burn my tongue.

"This is our last taste of the easy life for a little while," Santiago said. "Once we leave in the morning, we'll have a couple of nights out on our own before we reach the comfort of Camp One around 18,000 feet."

I still couldn't believe I was here and that tomorrow I would be setting foot on the mountain.

"Oh, Riley! I almost forgot. I have a gift for you." He quickly left the tent and returned a moment later. He handed me a small rectangular package wrapped in brown paper.

"Thank you," I said as I untied the yellow twine.

Inside was a book bound with a leather cover. I opened it up and saw the pages were blank. It was a journal. Inside the front cover were two HB pencils and a tiny sharpener, the kind I had as a child.

"That was unexpected—thank you," I said.

"It's a place to record your thoughts, and of course your dreams on the mountain."

"I'm afraid I don't dream much, or if I do, I sure don't remember them in the morning," I said.

"Here on the mountain, dreams carry important messages from the soul. Whenever you have one, try to write it down in the morning and we can talk about it when we climb."

Just then someone's footsteps could be heard approaching the tent from outside.

"That must be Osvaldo," said Santiago.

The long zipper of the cook tent began opening from the bottom until a figure emerged through the doorway. He was wearing a black snow hat with a headlamp and a puffy gray down-filled jacket.

"Todo bien?" said Santiago, smiling as he stood up to give Osvaldo a hug. Osvaldo looked to be in his mid-thirties. He was short and stocky, and his dark leathery skin told me he spent most of his time outside.

"Hola," I said, standing to greet him. Osvaldo smiled back politely. The two men talked briefly in Spanish before Osvaldo turned to wave goodbye and disappeared into the night.

"He didn't stay long," I remarked.

"No, but he's a beautiful soul," said Santiago. "He doesn't say much, and I don't think he knows more than ten words in English. But we couldn't climb this mountain without him."

"I'm glad he's here then. You know, if someone had told me a few days ago that I would be sitting in a base camp, about to climb a mountain, I would have told them they're crazy."

"Isn't life beautiful?" Santiago said, smiling.

43

Cemetery of Souls

"Not quite the word I'd choose, but what the heck, here we are."

I was exhausted from the long hike today and wanted to get some sleep. "I think it's time for me to go. I want to be fresh for tomorrow," I said, gathering my things to head back to my tent.

"Riley," Santiago said before I could leave. "There's something you need to know." His voice, now serious, told me it was time to sit back down. "You're about to embark on the adventure of a lifetime, but it will be one of the most difficult things you ever do."

"I know," I said.

"But … there's something you need to know. Once you set foot on that mountain tomorrow, there's no turning back."

"What do you mean?"

"The only option is to keep climbing."

"What if bad weather moves in, or there's an accident?" I asked.

"There's no turning back," he repeated, this time more sternly. "You must go all the way to the summit. Do you understand?"

"I think so. But what happens if I can't do it? You know I've never climbed a mountain before."

Santiago looked at me with concern. "If you quit, there would be a soul death."

"A what?" I asked.

"A death of the soul," he answered quietly. "You've been summoned here for an appointment. But if you leave, your soul will withdraw into the shadows, no longer seeking its unique expression, but instead resigning itself to a numb and unfulfilled life. This is a soul death."

44

The Call to Climb

The air in the tent grew heavy.

"And we would place a plaque with your name on it, on top of the cairn along the path."

"Wait ... the people whose names are on those plaques didn't actually die? They were just the ones who turned back?" I asked.

"Yes," said Santiago. "But those plaques were not for the people. They were for their souls. That's who we honored today. The parts of them that gave up, that lost their voice."

"That's so sad. But maybe they can try again," I said. "Maybe they weren't ready."

"No," he said gravely. "They can never come back. Their soul has quit speaking, and no longer tries to get their attention. In fact, the people themselves no longer have any recollection that they were here."

"They don't remember?" I asked, trying to wrap my head around what that meant.

Santiago stood and zipped up his jacket. "No, Riley ... they don't. So before you step on the mountain tomorrow, understand that once you do, there's no turning back."

With that, he disappeared into the night.

I sat frozen, fear heavy in my heart. I had quit so many times—projects, relationships, even my business—and each time I promised myself I'd do better next time. But this was different. The death of my soul? I needed to think about this ... but I was almost out of time.

I returned to my tent and crawled into my sleeping bag, feeling like the mountain itself was pressing down on me. As I lay there and tried to clear my thoughts, all I could hear was the wind whistling softly, sending ripples through the walls of my tent, which answered back with a steady flip-flapping of nylon fabric. The two together created the simplest of symphonies as they traded notes in a strangely hypnotic performance. I lay motionless in the dark, listening. As I turned my attention inward, I felt a stirring, but of what? And as the conversation between the wind and my tent drifted into the background, a new one was beginning: a conversation between me and my soul.

Key Takeaways from Section I

1. **The Importance of Alignment:** When your life is out of alignment with your soul's intent, it can manifest as dissatisfaction, restlessness, or even a crisis.

2. **Answering the Call:** Challenges and unexpected events are sometimes life's way of getting your attention and calling you to adjust your path. These moments are opportunities for growth and transformation.

3. **The Soul versus the Ego:** Your soul seeks meaning and authenticity, while your ego prioritizes safety and approval. Recognizing this inner conflict is essential to living intentionally.

4. **The Summons of the Soul:** Your soul desires to have a conversation with you so that you might understand its intent and thus fulfill your destiny.

For more resources from Section I, visit:
www.iwillclimb.com/summons

Section II

Honor Your Path

"When the path is right, the energy is there."
— *Dr. James Hollis*

Chapter 6

Copy and Paste

Elevation 13,121 feet

I awoke to the sound of Santiago's voice outside my tent. It was still dark and bitterly cold. My body groaned at the thought of leaving the warm and cozy sleeping bag. Instead, I tried to get dressed inside the bag. It wasn't easy, but it was better than stepping out into the cold.

In the cook tent, a hearty breakfast of sausages, beans, and avocado was waiting for me. After downing a second cup of coffee, we each packed up our tents and sleeping bags and stuffed them into our packs.

"Where's Osvaldo?" I asked. "His tent is gone."

"He went ahead to fix some ropes on the glacier, so they'll be ready for us when we get there," said Santiago.

While we made our final preparations, I knew we were only minutes away from setting foot on the mountain. If I was going to back out, I had better speak up now. I looked around at Santiago and the two young porters, packing and organizing supplies. *Wow*, I thought, *all these people out here in the cold, just to help me.* It plucked a string of guilt in my stomach. If I quit now, what would they think? I also didn't want a plaque with my name on it, hanging on some cairn. I felt trapped between not wanting to disappoint everyone, and the fear of failing if I tried. As if he could read my mind, Santiago approached.

"Riley, are you ready?"

"Well, I hope so…. I'm scared actually." There was nothing to hide now.

"I know. But you're going to be okay. Just remember, the key to climbing any mountain is 'one more step.' That's it. When you think you can't do it and you want to go back down, I just want you to take one more step. Okay?"

I nodded.

"Eventually, there'll be no more steps to take." He placed his hand on my shoulder. "When you're ready, let's climb."

I walked to the edge of camp and stopped at the base of the mountain. This was my last chance to back out. One more step meant risking everything. Santiago stood behind me, patiently waiting.

One more step, Riley, I said to myself, and after a deep breath, the sole of my boot touched down on the slope of La Montaña. The climb was on.

It was still dark as our headlamps unveiled the path one step at a time.

"Today we're going to climb up this ravine that's in front of us and then make our way onto the glacier," said Santiago as he pointed up the mountain.

As the sky began to illuminate to the east, the silhouettes of the surrounding peaks appeared. The reality of the climb

52

The Call to Climb

began to settle in and then I remembered my dream from last night. I'm not sure why it hadn't come to me when I first woke up. "Last night I had a dream," I said, trying to keep up with Santiago.

"Really? And what do you remember?"

"It was weird. I was waiting for a train. It was one of those outdoor stations like you see in Europe and I was the only one there. I was worried I was in the wrong place. So I checked my ticket, which had been in my pocket, but all the ink was smudged and I couldn't read anything. Then I heard the train approaching and when it rounded the bend, it was old, like the kind you see in movies about the Old West. As it got close, I could see that it was run down, like it had been neglected. The paint was peeling in many places and the colors were dull."

Santiago stopped and turned to look at me.

"I boarded and sat down but there was no one else on the train. And as it left the station, I remember looking out the window. The land was barren, almost like it was winter but without any snow. Finally, the train came to its first stop, and I looked outside to see who might be getting on. But the platform was empty; there was no one. Then I realized it was the same station from where I had boarded the train earlier. I was confused and worried that I might be on the wrong train, so I decided to talk to the person who was driving. I walked to the front of the car and knocked on the door, but no one answered. So I opened it and found there was no one in the cockpit. It was like a ghost train, and I was afraid it was going to crash, and that's the last thing I remember. Weird, huh?" I finished.

"Dreams only seem weird when we don't know what they're telling us," Santiago said, as he turned and continued up the trail.

"So what do you think it means?" I asked.

"You'll know the meaning when it comes to you," he said, as he continued up the path.

"I thought you had some special powers of dream interpretation," I half-joked.

Santiago laughed. "Well, I do have some powers," he said. "I have the power to predict the future."

"I wouldn't be surprised," I said, laughing.

"Fair enough. But let me prove it to you. Ten days from now, when you look up into the night sky, it will be filled with shooting stars."

"Really?" I asked. "Is this a magical mountain kind of thing?"

"No, it's going to happen all over the world. Millions of people will see it, but I'm just predicting it now."

"Okay, so how do you know that?"

"Because it's a meteor shower, Riley, and it happens every year on the same night."

"Ha, that's cheating," I said. "I've actually heard of that. I forget the name but, yes, my friend invited me once to go watch it. But that's not really predicting the future."

"Really? Why not? It's an event that is going to happen in the future, and I just told you about it."

"Nice try. But I think the credit goes to the Earth's orbit on this one."

"Touché, Riley, but this actually has a lot to do with your dream. You're correct about the meteor shower, the Perseids. Every year the Earth collides with them on precisely the same night.

We can predict it because we're traveling in a loop, and loops repeat themselves. It's the same with life. There was a woman not long ago who had been summoned here to climb. She worked for a charity and had been faithfully journaling almost every day for twelve years. But one day after writing she decided to look back over some of the previous entries she'd made from that same day in years past. At first she thought it might be a nice stroll down memory lane, until she uncovered something … disturbing."

Santiago stopped and turned to face me.

"She noticed that some of the entries from previous years were eerily similar to what she had just written. At first she thought it was a coincidence but the more she read, the more she saw. Certain days had the same thoughts, the same struggles, the same fears. Other days were filled with resolve and determination to change. She even found she was getting sick in the same week in successive years! It struck her then—her life felt like a copy and paste, each year repeating itself with only minor edits, as if she were stuck in an endless loop of familiarity."

"Whoa," I said. "That's freaky."

"It is, but it's not," he said. "You see, people live their lives in patterns, large loops, repeating over and over. It turns out we're not much different from the Earth and how it orbits around the sun. But the problem with these loops is they're so big that by the time you get back to where you started, you don't realize that you've been there before. There's no yearly meteor shower to make you stop and say, 'Hey wait a minute, I've seen this before.' But that's what the woman's journal was. It was a window that revealed the patterns of her life."

55

Copy and Paste

"I wonder why she couldn't see it," I asked. "That doesn't make sense to me."

"Riley, it's not just that woman. It's everyone. No one gets up in the morning and says to themselves, 'Today I'm going to make the same stupid mistakes, and give into the same fears that sabotage my potential,' but then they do. Because everyone's life follows a set of patterns. They just don't see them."

"The train in my dream! Oh, my goodness, it brought me back to the same station, which means I was traveling in a loop!"

Santiago nodded.

I stood there for a moment, thinking. "But I don't think I'm living in a loop. If I was, I'm pretty sure I'd see it."

"It's easier to see patterns in others than it is to see your own. Like a fish, it doesn't know it's wet. If I asked a few of your closest friends, they could tell me some of your patterns. But make no mistake, everything in your life is the result of your patterns of behavior, both your successes and your shortcomings," said Santiago, as he paused to let me absorb what he said. "People may live eighty years, but in reality, they often live only one year, repeated eighty times."

His words stung a bit but also irritated me. I thought about my recent business failure, which wasn't my fault, and some of the hard times working with Rick. None of those had anything to do with my patterns.

Santiago stopped once again and turned to me. "Here's the sobering truth, Riley. Once you begin to see your patterns … you can then predict your future."

"What do you mean?" I asked.

56

The Call to Climb

"The woman with the journal," he said. "The more she looked, she discovered there were clear patterns in her relationships, her job, and even her love life. And the moment she saw them, she gained the power to look into her future. It was like unwrapping her very own crystal ball."

"Really? How did you come to that conclusion?" I asked.

"Because the best predictors of future behavior are the patterns of the past."

"That sounds depressing," I said. "Almost as if she's bound by fate and can never change."

"The truth is not depressing, Riley. The truth has the power to set you free. Her patterns from the past showed her what the future would likely be, unless ..."

Santiago paused and leaned closer as if to tell me a secret. "Unless she made the conscious choice to interrupt the patterns that were defining her life. Only then could she dislodge the train from the track, so to speak, and carve out the life she wanted to live, rather than the life she was living. In your dream last night, your soul was telling you that you're living in a loop and it's out of alignment with who you're meant to be. Why do you think the landscape in the dream was so barren?"

"Okay, supposing that's true, how does someone change this? How do I get the train onto a better track?" I asked.

"Great question," he said. "We'll get to that later, but first, look." He pointed up the mountain. There, seated on a large boulder, was a smiling Osvaldo.

The sun was now peaking over the ridge to the east, creating a spectacular sunrise. Osvaldo had been waiting at the edge of the glacier. I'd never seen one up close before. It stretched out

57

Copy and Paste

before me like a massive, frozen expanse, its jagged surface shimmering in shades of deep blue and white. The ice seemed alive, with cracks and crevices. It was both beautiful and intimidating, like a field of shattered glass frozen in time.

"Wow, that looks beautiful," I said.

"Yes, it's time to gear up," responded Santiago.

Osvaldo had an open bag of climbing gear waiting for us. He handed me a harness to put on and a set of crampons to attach to my boots. They looked menacing with the sharp metal teeth jutting out from the bottoms of my feet.

He then took a long rope and gave one end to Santiago and kept the other for himself. Then he clipped me into the middle. It was my first rope team.

"We'll cross the icefield roped together for safety. If someone falls into a crevasse, the other two will need to arrest their fall," said Santiago. "But you're missing one crucial thing, Riley. Your ice axe." As if on cue, Osvaldo appeared from behind and handed me a shiny silver ice axe. It looked deadly, with a long, pointed spike on one end and what looked like a small upside-down shovel on the other.

"Whoa, you could hurt someone with this," I said, as I waved it about.

I felt powerful with it in my hand.

"Riley, I need to tell you something very important. On the glacier there are many crevasses. Some might be covered with snow so that we don't see them. If I suddenly disappear because I've stepped into one, you fall to the ground and jab the long point of your axe into the ice. Osvaldo will do the same and the

58

The Call to Climb

two of you will act as anchors to keep me from falling all the way to the bottom. On the mountain, we're all in this together."

"Okay, got it," I said. "But how deep are these crevasses?"

"Hard to say. But they can easily go a couple hundred feet."

"That's terrifying," I said. I was astonished.

We began making our way across the ice flow. My crampons chewed into the ice with a loud crunching sound. The grip was amazing. I'd never felt so stable on ice before.

After about thirty minutes, Santiago stopped. "Okay, we're here," he said. Knowing what to do, Osvaldo took off his pack and began fixing two large ice screws about three feet apart, deep into the ice.

"Where are we?" I asked.

"Think of it as a scenic rest stop," he smiled. "I want to show you something. Come here for a moment and look down there."

I stepped up beside him and looked down to where he was pointing. A few feet away was an opening in the ice that descended into the dark.

"Whoa, I wouldn't want to fall down there," I said.

"No, you wouldn't, but we'll be okay. We'll be roped and Osvaldo will stay up here as an anchor."

"Wait, we're going down there?"

"Yes, it'll be fun."

Before I could protest, Santiago double-checked my harness and gave Osvaldo a thumbs-up.

"Just trust the rope, Riley, Osvaldo will always have you. But before we go down, I want to revisit the dream you had on the train."

59

Copy and Paste

"Uh, sure," I said, a bit confused as to why he'd bring this up now.

"You said you walked to the front and opened the door to the engine room. Do you remember who was driving?"

"Yeah, no one," I said.

"At least no one you could see," Santiago replied. "But you're about to discover who that is."

Chapter 7

Beneath the Ice

Elevation 14,377 feet

We began our descent into the crevasse. The slope was steep, but my crampons cut into the ice with each step. The sounds from the surface soon disappeared as we ventured farther down into the belly of the glacier. As the passageway narrowed, Santiago turned on his headlamp and we continued to descend. The farther we went, the more claustrophobic I began to feel.

"Are we supposed to be down here?" I asked.

"We're almost there," he said. Then he stopped. "Do you hear that?" I halted my descent to listen.

A faint gurgling noise echoed up from the darkness. "That sounds like water," I said.

"Yes, not much farther."

We descended another minute until the passage widened into a large cavern. A couple of winding shafts in the ceiling funneled sunlight from the surface so that the entire chamber could be seen without a headlamp. The walls of solid ice must have been thirty feet high and were translucent and blue. The air down here felt warmer than up on the surface. Flowing out of one wall was a small stream. It was the purest water I'd ever seen as it trickled past our feet, filling the chamber with soft echoes.

"Wow. This place is incredible," I said.

"It's one of a kind," said Santiago. "If we returned in a month, it wouldn't exist."

"Why's that?"

"Because the glacier is always moving. It's basically a gigantic river of ice that travels down this mountain a few inches every day."

"So that's why you say this room will be gone in a month?"

"Yes, it could even be gone tomorrow."

Santiago must have read my face. "Don't worry. It's early morning, so the glacier is still frozen. But as the sun heats it, the ice will start to move. That's when we don't want to be down here."

I scanned the icy room, trying to take it in.

Santiago unclipped from the rope and walked over to one of the walls. He took out his axe and chipped off a small fragment of ice. "Take a look at this," as he walked over and placed it in my glove. "This piece of ice is almost a hundred thousand years old."

"You've gotta be kidding me."

"Not only that, but trapped inside it is a snapshot from the day it was frozen. That's why scientists like to study glaciers, because the ice contains a memory of what was happening in the past."

I was in awe as I examined it. I still felt like we shouldn't be here, but at the same time, I didn't want to leave.

"You asked me earlier how to change the patterns in your life. Well, if you want to change your patterns, you must go to the source, because all of your patterns are driven by something deeper—your programs."

"Programs?" I asked.

"Yes, programs, like the ones on your computer. But your programs are not made of binary code; instead, they're clusters of beliefs or stories that you've acquired over your lifetime. These stories now shape the way you see things."

"What things?" I asked.

"The way you see yourself, and the way you see the world. All your beliefs will fall into one of those two categories," said Santiago. "Your programs create your patterns, and your patterns determine your life.

"Remember the woman with the journal? It was the same with her. All her repetitive behaviors were being driven by her programs. But can you see what the problem is?"

I thought for a moment, before answering. "I guess I would ask, how do I know what my programs are?"

"Yes, great question," he said. "Because the problem with your programs is that most of them live in your subconscious, deep down here below the surface. You don't even realize they're here." He paused to look around the cavern of ice where we stood.

"Ah ... so this is kind of like my subconscious?" I asked.

"Exactly," he said. "Just as the ice from this glacier has a memory of the past, your subconscious is a gigantic storage vault for everything that's happened in your life. It assembles

63

Beneath the Ice

all these events and tries to make sense of them by creating stories. These stories become the programs that drive your repetitive patterns.

"So the question is, Riley, are you living the life that you want? Or the life you're programmed to live?"

Then it hit me. "The train! This is why no one was driving the train!" I said excitedly. "Because it's my subconscious that I can't see!"

Santiago's face lit up with a huge smile as he nodded in agreement.

"So if I have programs in my subconscious, where did they come from?"

"A lot of them are formed in your first six or seven years of life, before you even knew what was happening. As Aristotle said, 'Give me the child until he is seven and I will show you the man.' Think of your earliest programs like a pair of glasses you were given that colored how you saw everything. But it wasn't only you. When you showed up on your first day of school, all your classmates were wearing glasses too, but each pair was different."

Thinking back, I was one of the lucky ones. I came from a good home. We weren't rich, but we weren't poor either. I didn't have a rough upbringing like so many people.

"But not all programming comes from our early life," he said. "Some is formed much later, even in adulthood, often shaped by painful experiences. It could be the betrayal of a partner, the loss of someone you love, or any moment that leaves a deep emotional scar. Whenever we experience significant pain, the subconscious creates new programming designed to protect

64

The Call to Climb

us—its sole aim is to ensure we never have to feel that kind of pain again."

"You said the goal of these programs is to keep us safe, but safe from what?" I asked.

"The short answer? Pain and survival threats—both physical and emotional. The ego and subconscious are wired to shield you from things like rejection by your tribe or the fear that you're unworthy of love. When you were a child, these protective programs made sense. You didn't yet have the strength or experience to navigate life on your own. Back then, they served you well. But as you've grown into adulthood, many of these programs have become outdated. Instead of protecting you, they now hold you back, keeping you from stepping fully into the life you're meant to live."

"This reminds me of the speech I was asked to give last year to a not-for-profit group. I dreaded it for weeks, and even lost sleep over it. I almost called them and canceled. But once it was over I remember asking myself why I had gotten so worked up."

Santiago laughed. "That's a great example of protective programming. Your subconscious believed that giving a speech was dangerous, and so it wanted you to back out. But the last time I checked, no one has ever died from giving a presentation. Good for you, Riley, for overriding the program."

"I can see how programs can create a conflict, like with my presentation."

"Yes, as I said before, your soul is not interested in the approval of the tribe. It only seeks to express its nature and fulfill its potential. On the other hand, the ego and the subconscious want you to play it safe, and this is sadly what the masses

65

Beneath the Ice

do—they mute the deeper desires within them and ignore the nudges from the soul."

I looked down at the piece of ice still in my glove, trying to grasp how this tiny chunk of frozen water contained a memory from a time before humans walked the earth. I also felt overwhelmed at how extensive the network of programming seemed to be in our lives.

"Come, let's go a little farther," Santiago said. "I can tell by the sound of the water that there's another chamber farther down."

I hesitated but followed. The stream led us through a crack in the far wall, and as we continued to descend, the passageway narrowed, forcing us to bend over in places as we moved forward. I felt my chest tighten. At any moment these giant slabs of ice could slide across and crush us forever.

A moment later the narrow passage opened again, this time into another chamber, no larger than a bedroom. The water trickled down and came to rest in a shallow pool in the center. The only light came from our headlamps, which cast long, eerie silhouettes of our bodies on the walls of ice.

I stood over the shallow pool, its surface reflecting the beams of light from my headlamp. In the crystal water, I saw my face staring back at me. I wondered what I might find if I looked deeper—what stories lay buried in the innermost layers of my subconscious? That's when I heard it. A chilling whisper from within me. "Get out," it said. It was old and familiar.

"Are you okay?" Santiago asked.

"Yes, it's just a little spooky down here."

66

The Call to Climb

He crouched down beside me at the edge of the pool. "A few years ago, there was a man who was summoned to climb. His name was John, and his business was failing, even though he was extremely talented and had a proven product. Yet despite all of this, he was hurtling toward bankruptcy."

"I can relate with that one," I said. "So what was the problem?"

"He didn't know, which frustrated him. But after he learned about programs, he decided to become curious. When he did, he saw a clear pattern. Every time his business would start to grow, and his bank account along with it, he would take his foot off the gas and start tinkering with his business."

"What do you mean, tinkering?"

"He'd spend time redesigning his logo, rearranging the office, or he'd start creating another product, even though he had more products than he could sell. But eventually he'd run out of money, prompting a stress-filled panic to find new clients, and then the cycle would repeat all over again."

"It's like he was sabotaging his own business," I said.

"Yes. And what do you think was driving his patterns?" Santiago asked.

"A program?"

"Yes, exactly. You see, he'd grown up in a poor rural community and his parents had always struggled to get ahead. They often spoke negatively about rich people, accusing them of being greedy and taking advantage of others. This was how they saw the world. It was the pair of glasses they were used to wearing.

"Well, this created a story inside of him while he was just a boy. It was a story about money, but also about love and approval from his parents. When his bank account grew, he felt like he was becoming rich, the very kind of person his parents had despised. So he would subconsciously stop looking for new clients, distracting himself instead with other work, tinkering until his income returned to a level where he would not be at risk of rejection."

"Whoa ... that's deep," I said.

"Yes, it is," said Santiago. "But once he saw the pattern, and the outdated programs driving it, he could now make better decisions that were more aligned with his soul. In other words, he brought what was below the surface into the light. If he hadn't, they would have remained unconscious, and what is unconscious becomes your master."

"What do you mean, 'becomes your master'?"

"Because if you don't know something is driving your behavior, then you will never address it, and it will therefore continue to run your life."

This whole conversation was beginning to feel heavy to me. "What I don't understand is why would his subconscious work against him?"

"Remember yesterday on the trail when we spoke about the soul and your ego? The ego is like the safety officer always trying to keep you in line with the rules. The subconscious is the rule book full of outdated policies. But the soul is the artist who doesn't want to follow the rules. It wants to create; it wants to fulfill its destiny. So yes, sometimes the ego and the subconscious are working against the soul, but it's because they simply want to protect you, because to them, the soul can at times seem reckless and threatening."

68

The Call to Climb

"The soul sounds like a badass," I said.

Santiago smiled. "Well, I've never heard anyone explain it like that before, but yes." He laughed. "The soul is badass. But the protective programs that are stored in your subconscious are immensely powerful, like this glacier. It seems to lie dormant here, yet it carves out valleys and levels entire mountains. People like to think they're in control of their lives, but they don't realize there's a shadow government, a 'deep state' if you will, that works behind the scenes to heavily influence your life. Because as soon as you decide to step out of your comfort zone, and step into a life that's more aligned with your soul, you will face heavy sanctions. It's the subconscious's way of keeping you in line."

"That sounds rather ominous," I said. "What do you mean by sanctions?"

"Fear and anxiety mostly. So when you try to live more authentically, you'll likely suffer these same punishments, all of which are designed to return you to the safe path set out by the ego and the subconscious."

The more he spoke, the more I began to see how prevalent fear and anxiety were in my life. Anyone who knew me would never have guessed. The image I projected on the outside was vastly different from the fears and doubts that haunted me from within.

"I have to be honest," I confessed. "All of this feels so heavy, depressing even. Maybe it's because I'm standing inside a massive glacier, feeling small, but what chance does a person like me have of changing? If my ego is tapping into powerful subconscious programs that I can't see, and these programs are driving my life, then how can I change? How can anyone change? Or is this just my lot in life and the sooner I accept it, the better?"

Just then a sharp crack echoed through the cavern, like the glacier itself had split open. I felt the shockwave in my chest.

"What was that?" I asked, my voice rising in pitch.

"That's the glacier waking up. Which means it's time for us to head back to the surface," said Santiago, calm as ever. "You've asked some great questions, Riley. The good news is, yes, you can change your programs. But let's continue this conversation up in the light."

As we began our ascent out of the dark, the weight of his words settled deeper within me. I was beginning to see that this journey was more than a climb—it was a reckoning with everything I'd hidden beneath the surface.

70

The Call to Climb

Chapter 8

The Examined Life

Elevation 14,377 feet

As we resurfaced, it took a moment to be able to open my eyes. The sun's reflection on the glacier was blinding. Osvaldo handed me a pair of dark glacier goggles, allowing me to open my eyes again.

"Nice glasses. Are they yours?" Santiago said with a sly grin.

"No, Osvaldo gave them to …" It took me a second to get the joke. "Come to think of it, these glasses make the world look different. You seem funnier," I quipped.

"Touché, Riley."

We finished crossing the glacier and began hiking up another ravine of black rock. It was slow going. Some of the boulders were the size of my washing machine back home, requiring us to jump up onto our stomachs before pulling the rest of the body up from there. The wind picked up and whipped our faces as we climbed. It was miserable.

By late afternoon, we reached the base of a massive rock face that rose above us hundreds of feet. A large overhang provided shelter from the wind where the three of us took a break for some food. It was the first time I'd stopped to see the view behind me, which was magnificent. We'd gained a lot of altitude. Even the glacier we'd crossed now seemed like a tiny white patch below us.

"That ice cave was crazy," I said. "But you still haven't answered my question. If these subconscious programs are driving my life, how do I know what they are?"

"It's a bit like being an archaeologist," he said. "How do they know where to dig? They must pay attention to the clues up here on the surface. It's not much different with the subconscious. The secret is to start looking, and you do that by living a more examined life."

"I thought I was pretty self-aware, but now I'm starting to think this requires a whole other level."

Santiago nodded. "The fact that you're on this mountain means you've taken the first steps, but to live in alignment with your soul, and not your programs, you have to first see your patterns. This takes curiosity without judgment."

Santiago stood up and put on his pack. "Let's talk while we climb. We still have a way to go."

"We're not going up there, are we?" I asked, looking up at the sheer cliff above us.

"No, we're going around it, so we'll spend a few hours walking along the base."

The trail was straight across, which was a relief from the uphill climb we'd had most of the day.

"An examined life, Riley, means becoming mindful of how you live. It's the only way you'll see the patterns and reflexes that are driven from below. Your conscious mind only runs

72

The Call to Climb

about five percent of the show, while the other ninety-five percent is the autopilot of the subconscious. So it takes deliberate effort to start paying attention to your actions, your emotions, and even your body."

"What's my body have to do with this?"

"A lot," he said. "When you called your boss from the village, did you notice how your body changed, how it constricted and tensed up?"

"Really? I had no idea, but I'm not surprised."

"That was your body reacting to your programs. The more you examine your life, the more you'll notice those things. It's like starting to see the annual meteor shower, which you never noticed was there because you hadn't looked up.

"A great way to start is by asking questions, like these: Why do I repeat the same mistakes? Why is it so hard for me to speak up? Why does my body tense up when my boss enters the room? The more curious you are, the more you begin to see."

"I'm not sure if you'd call this a pattern, but one of the things I'm terrible at is saying no. There are so many times where I've said yes to something that I didn't want to do at all."

"Good one, Riley, yes exactly. Once you see a pattern like that, it's time to find out what program is driving it. What story are you telling yourself that keeps you repeating the behavior? Remember, there's always a reason that makes sense to the subconscious. So a great question to ask yourself is 'What is this in service to?' or another way to think about it, 'What is the payoff, or the reward, I get from doing this?'

"Remember John, the business owner? After he saw his pattern of sabotaging his business every time he had too much money in his account, he started asking questions. 'Why do I lose my desire to sell more after my bank account reaches a certain number? What's the payoff for doing this?' Now here's the thing. When you haven't done this before, the answers don't come right away. But the more he quieted his mind and reflected, the subconscious eventually revealed what he needed to know."

"I feel like I've asked myself a million times why I can never say no. But there's never been an obvious answer."

"Do you ask that question out of anger and frustration? Or later, when your mind is quiet, and you have time to listen?"

I laughed. "It's usually right after I hang up the phone, kicking myself for agreeing to watch my friend's puppy for the long weekend. That's when."

Santiago smiled at me. "I'm glad you love animals," he said. "It's a sign of a good soul. But here's the thing. If you want to hear from the subconscious, you can't go in like a SWAT team, kicking down the door and demanding answers, which brings me to the second principle of an examined life, and that's to detach from judgment."

"This should be good for me to hear. I've been known to beat myself up a few times a week."

"So what's the payoff for always saying yes?"

"Payoff? Other than me staying inside all weekend, cleaning up pee from my carpet, I can't think of any." I laughed sarcastically.

Santiago stopped and put down his pack. "Have a seat," he said.

The Call to Climb

"Let's try something. I'm going to ask you a series of questions. Pretend I'm just a voice in your head."

"Okay, sure," I laughed.

"When's the last time you said yes when you should have said no?"

"It's actually the puppy incident. That was a real story that happened three weeks ago, with Sara, my coworker."

"Okay, perfect. So why did you say yes?" asked Santiago.

"I'm not sure. I think I just felt uncomfortable saying no. See, I'm no good at this."

"Relax, Riley," he said calmly. "There are no wrong answers. Now, why did you feel uncomfortable?"

"I guess ... I didn't want her to be upset with me."

"Okay, good, and why didn't you want her to be upset with you?"

"Because I don't like the feeling of conflict," I said.

"And why don't you like the feeling of conflict?"

"I don't know. I mean, who likes conflict ... I'm not sure what to tell you."

I felt frustrated by the questions and like a loser that I couldn't answer them better.

"Riley," he said in his calm voice, "close your eyes for a moment and take a deep breath."

I did as he asked, trying not to feel stupid.

"Now, why don't you like the feeling of conflict?"

"Because when people are angry with you, they might turn others against you too."

I opened my eyes. "Did I just say that?"

75

The Examined Life

Santiago nodded. "Your subconscious just gave you a gift—a story from down below."

"That's wild. I would have never connected the dots."

"At some point in your life, you created this story, that when people are angry with you, they might turn others against you too. Now imagine, Riley, if we wrote a children's book and that was the moral of the story?"

"Oh, my goodness." I laughed. "That would be terrible."

"That's the story you've been telling yourself for a long time, and the payoff for always saying yes is to protect you from your social circle turning on you."

"Wow, that's pathetic actually," I said.

Santiago looked at me with one eyebrow raised.

"Right … nonjudgment. Got it."

"That's a micro example of living an examined life. When you sit with the questions, you'll begin to peel back the layers and get closer to the root cause, which is often a story that's buried deep in your subconscious."

"I would imagine you could uncover some pretty ugly truths," I said.

"They're not ugly, Riley. They're just programs trying to protect you. But if you're afraid of what you'll uncover, or if you want to judge them, or yourself for that matter, then your subconscious will resist offering up the answers. No one wants to open the door when someone is pounding on the other side."

Santiago picked up his backpack again and slung it over his back. "Let's keep climbing."

As we walked over the next hour, I reflected on the exercise with Santiago. *What other stuff is buried down there?* I wondered. But there was something still bothering me.

"Santiago, I have a question. Just because we uncovered a story doesn't mean it's going to fix anything, does it?"

"An excellent insight, Riley. And you're right, awareness only buys you a ticket into the stadium. It's down on the field where the real work begins. The key to changing the program is to change the story, or the belief. Let's go back to John for a moment. Once he saw the story he was telling himself, which was basically, 'If I'm rich, then I'm one of those bad people who take advantage of others, and my parents will disown me,' the next step was to write a new story—one that aligned with own his values and beliefs, not those of his parents. He knew his business was blessing lives and that a bulging bank account was a good thing, plus an opportunity to help even more. He also knew that his parents loved him and hadn't disowned him after many of the crazy things he'd done throughout his life."

"And that was it?" I asked. "That seems a little too simple."

Santiago smiled, "It was only the beginning. If someone has been telling themselves a story for years, it takes a little time. It's a bit like changing a habit. Not only that, but some of our stories also come with an emotional charge. This makes them even more stubborn to dislodge."

"You lost me there. What's an emotional charge?"

"It's one thing to change a simple belief, like you thought you needed a master's degree to apply for this job, but it turns out you don't. It's a simple correction. But when the belief has higher stakes, like in this case, 'If I become too wealthy, I could be rejected by my primary caregivers,' then the subconscious is going to resist more when letting it go. Because, to the subconscious, there's risk. You must prove that it's safe to let the story go, and this doesn't happen in five minutes. Have you ever seen a small child hold on to a toy, and they don't want to give it up?"

"Oh yeah. My little nephew. He has these vice grips for hands."

"You can probably reason with him for an hour, but he won't let go until he's ready, until he feels like it. The subconscious can be like that. But to be fair, your subconscious is not your enemy. Imagine if Osvaldo and I told you that you're going to scale this cliff above us, but without any ropes. How are you going to feel about that?"

I looked up at the sheer wall above us. "Ha, not a chance! I would die for sure."

Santiago laughed. "That's probably the exact words your subconscious uses when you ask it to surrender a story that it believes has kept you alive all these years.

"So even though John began to tell himself that money wasn't a threat to his relationship with his parents, the real test came when his bank account began to grow. Because he was living a more examined life, he caught the first inklings of anxiety when he saw that his bank balance was approaching an all-time high.

"In the past, he wouldn't have noticed, and the programs would have taken over. But now he was able to remind himself of the new story and continue to focus on sales despite the anxiety."

"So his anxiety was still there?"

"Yes, at first. But over time it diminished as the subconscious finally let go. It was a process. Step by step, just like climbing a mountain."

"So what happened to his business?" I asked.

"The last I heard it was wildly successful. He's helping more people than he ever imagined, and recently he flew his parents to Italy. His mom had always dreamed of seeing Venice, and she finally got to."

"Wow. That's the kind of life I want."

"If you remember, before we ever set foot on this mountain, I told you that the soul's path is filled with obstacles, including powerful forces from within. This is what I was talking about. To truly live in alignment with your soul, you must be willing to do the work. This is why you must live an examined life."

It was getting late in the day and my legs were spent. Santiago pointed to a small ledge up ahead that was protected by the overhang. "We'll camp up there tonight."

The overhang felt like the entrance to a cave, without the shelter of one. There was just enough room to fit all three of our tents. Osvaldo got out the stove and made us a dinner of pasta and some kind of meat. It was simple but delicious.

"How are you feeling?" Santiago asked. "It was your first official day on the mountain."

"I learned a lot," I said. "And I have a lot to think about."

I paused for a moment, weighing my next comment. "If I'm honest, all of this feels heavy."

"Tell me more," he said.

The Examined Life

"This idea of living in alignment with the soul sounds so appealing, but then you see what you're up against—the ego, the subconscious, my own weakness."

I paused for a moment, hoping I hadn't hurt his feelings.

"I don't know, maybe I'm just tired but sometimes I feel—discouraged. I've tried to change my life many times in the past, and if I'm radically honest, I don't know that I'm much different."

I was waiting for Santiago to respond, but he didn't, which made me feel worse. Instead, the three of us just sat in silence, staring out over the moonlit valley below.

Finally, he spoke. "Riley, most people wait for permission from someone else to live their life," he said. "But it's never granted. Permission to live your life is not something you seek; it's something you must seize. To do this there needs to be a change in government, an overthrow of the ego, and an uprising of the soul. Only then can you make new choices, and chart new paths. This is why you're here. This is why you've been called to climb. And tomorrow, we're going to take one more big step."

Chapter 9

The Gift

Elevation 15,274 feet

The wind was gentler tonight, weaving softly through the walls of my tent. I lay still on my thin sleeping pad, staring up at the faint outline of the fabric ceiling. My body ached from the climb, but my mind buzzed with everything Santiago had said over the past few days. The pieces were slowly coming together into something I still couldn't quite name yet but it felt significant—like I was closer to an answer I hadn't known I was seeking.

When I woke up the next morning I didn't want to leave the warmth of my sleeping bag. There was nothing fun about the next hour, and as I got dressed, my body protested. I walked outside and sat on a cold rock beside the stove. A dense fog had rolled in sometime over the night. Osvaldo smiled and handed me a cup of coffee, for which I was grateful. For the next twenty minutes I sat, shivering.

We packed up our gear and hit the trail. The fog completely enveloped the mountain, revealing the path in front of us only a few feet at a time. My knees felt like glass as I stumbled along the uneven rock.

"Last night, I was thinking about what you said about changing our programs. But then I started wondering . . . there must be hundreds of them. A person could work on this every day and never change them all."

"The goal isn't to change every program you have," Santiago said, glancing back at me. "The goal is to live in alignment with your soul. The focus is always forward. When you find areas where your subconscious programming gets in the way, that's where the work lies."

"That's a relief to hear," I said. "So how do I figure out what my soul really wants?" I asked.

The concept sounded motivational at first, but trying to make it practical still seemed a mystery to me.

"I've always felt this pull toward something bigger, but I can never seem to grasp it. I've started so many projects—ideas that, at the time, felt like they were my calling. But they all failed. How do I find my purpose?"

"By listening," he said as he continued to climb up the path in front of me.

"Listening?" I echoed, confused. "Well, I'd like to know soon, because I'm pretty sure I'm getting fired when I get home, and I want to know what job I should be looking for," I said.

"Your purpose isn't dependent on a job or some project— it's like a thread that weaves through your entire life, through every choice you've made, every experience. It's subtle but always there."

"So it's not a job or a task I do?"

"No, because what happens when you complete the task? Then your purpose would be over. Tasks exist within your purpose, but your purpose itself is not a box to check."

"I get what you're saying, but that doesn't help me right now. It's so vague. Don't you have some steps I can follow to find out what I'm supposed to do?"

Santiago stopped and turned toward me. "You're missing the point. You're searching for what you're 'supposed to do,' instead of asking who you're supposed to be. Do you remember when I told you the soul is like the seed of an oak tree?"

"Yes, on the trail into base camp," I said.

"The seed desires to become an oak tree. That's its destiny. As an oak tree it will 'do' many things—provide shade, make homes for animals—but those things happen because of what it is. Your soul is like that. It desires for you to grow into the highest expression of yourself. But the focus is on who you are, not what you do."

I stood there listening, as he spoke. The fog had erased the mountain completely, leaving us in some surreal place.

"So my purpose is not about doing anything, but just being me?" I asked skeptically.

"Exactly," Santiago said. "To be the most honest, authentic version of yourself. That's your gift to the world. And when you're walking that path, the energy will be there. Don't think of your purpose as something to accomplish—it's more like a song you're meant to play, and no one else can play it. The world has never heard anything like it, and that's why you're here."

"If the gift I bring to the world is me being myself, then I feel bad for the world," I joked. "Sort of like being the kid at

83

The Gift

your rich friend's birthday party, and all you brought was the cheap dollar-store present."

Santiago didn't respond, as if letting me digest my own comment. Then he turned and started climbing again.

I hurried to catch up.

"That's different from everything I've heard about finding purpose," I said. "I went to a workshop once where they had us do various assessments to help us figure out what career we should pursue."

Santiago stopped again, "There was a woman who found her passion speaking from the stage. She loved that she was impacting thousands of lives each week. She believed fully that this was what she was born to do, that it was her calling. But after speaking so much she damaged her vocal cords, and they had to operate. The operation wasn't successful, and she lost her voice entirely. Unable to speak anymore, she fell into a dark depression because she felt like her reason for living had been taken away. But she had confused her purpose with the activities of her job. Speaking on stage was just one vehicle for her soul to fulfill its destiny. There were countless others. The reason she was impacting lives was not because she was a speaker; it was because of who she was while she happened to be speaking.

"Over time, she found new ways to share her message. She turned to writing, pouring her words onto the page with the same passion she once spoke with. She mentored others one-on-one, guiding them in ways she previously didn't have time for. Eventually, she realized that losing her voice had forced her to discover a deeper truth—her purpose was never tied to a single act, but to the essence of who she was. And that could never be taken away."

I thought back to my life at home—the stress, the constant running, the feeling that I was chasing a life I didn't even want. How much of my time had been spent trying to be someone I wasn't? How often had I swallowed my truth to make others more comfortable? I was so busy trying to meet everyone's expectations that I'd stopped asking a simple question: *Who do I really want to be?*

"I think I understand but I was hoping for some clarity on what's next in my life, and where I should be focused," I said.

"Everyone needs a mountain to climb, Riley—a worthy pursuit."

What's that, a worthy pursuit?" I asked.

"Once you're clear on your purpose then you can 'do' things that are in alignment with that, whether it's a job, a project, or even a hobby. A worthy pursuit is what takes your purpose and creates meaning by impacting others. But we'll talk more about worthy pursuits higher up the mountain, I promise."

"That would be helpful."

"But for now, to live authentically, you need something deeper than goals or career paths. You need a vision."

"A vision?" I echoed.

He nodded. "A spiritual vision for your life."

"I'm not really a religious person," I said.

"It's not about that. A spiritual vision for your life is about who you want to show up as in the world—the person you aspire to be. It's not about perfection; it's about intention. It's about choosing to align your actions with your soul, day after day."

85

The Gift

The fog was slowly lifting as shapes of jagged peaks in the distance now appeared. Their silhouettes filled the horizon, like guardians watching over some sacred place. "I've never thought of it that way," I admitted.

"Most people don't," Santiago said. "They set goals about what they want to *do* but forget to ask who they want to *be*. That's where you make the difference to the world, Riley. If you're not convinced, consider this. One day you will die and at your funeral someone's going to take about a minute to read your eulogy about what you accomplished. Then the rest of the time will be people talking about who you were, and why you'll be missed."

He paused for a moment to let it sink in.

"Your spiritual vision answers the questions 'Who do you want to be? How do you want to show up? How do you want others to experience you? What kind of energy do you want to bring to the world?'"

"Okay, but what if I don't know the answers?"

Santiago smiled. "You can first start by getting clear on your values, but they need to be *your* values, not the values of others. Then think about the most important areas in your life, things like family, career, or health. For each area, ask yourself what you believe and why. Then write out your vision for each area. Your vision doesn't have to be grand. It simply has to be yours."

We continued climbing throughout the afternoon. The terrain was getting steeper but I felt like we were in a good rhythm. I kept to myself most of the day while I thought about my purpose. My life was so filled with trying to find the next big thing that I never stopped to consider who I wanted to be.

That night, after dinner, I sat alone in my tent with my notebook in my lap. The wind outside blew softly as I stared at the blank page in front of me. I thought about Santiago's words, about creating a spiritual vision for my life. *Who do I want to be?* I wrote the question at the top of the page.

I closed my eyes and imagined the person I wanted to show up as—the kind of person I'd be proud to meet at the end of my life. I also thought about my funeral. What would I want people to say about me?

Someone who lives with courage, who is strong but kind. Someone who inspires and gives people hope. A loyal friend. Not stressed out, but calm and confident. A person who is filled with optimism, and unshakable determination ...

The list grew as I kept writing. For the first time, I wasn't focused on accomplishments, or a dollar amount in my bank account, or chasing someone else's version of success. I was defining the person I truly wanted to become.

When I finished, I felt lighter—as if I'd just uncovered something I'd been carrying all along. Santiago's words came back to me: *Your purpose is like a song you play for the world that no one else can play.* I liked that.

Outside my tent, I heard Santiago's voice.

"Riley, is everything okay?" he asked.

I unzipped my door and leaned my head outside. "Yes," I said as I turned my book around so he could see.

As he crouched down to read what I wrote, he smiled. "This is your compass, Riley, When life gets overwhelming, when you feel lost, return to this vision. It will guide you back to yourself."

I nodded, feeling the truth of his words. "It's strange. I've spent so much of my life trying to prove myself, to feel successful. But when I think about showing up as this version of me … it feels like enough."

"Because it is," Santiago said gently. "Your soul doesn't need to *earn* worthiness. It simply needs to *express* itself. That's your purpose."

I took a deep breath, letting his words sink in. I felt a sense of peace wash over me. I didn't need to become anyone else. I just needed to become *me*.

"At the end of the day, your greatest gift to the world is *you*. The real you. Not the person shaped by fear or other people's expectations, but the soul-aligned, authentic version of yourself. When you create a spiritual vision for your life, you decide who you want to be, and from that place, everything else flows."

Santiago paused. His eyes blazed as they reflected the sun, which was setting over the jagged peaks on the horizon.

"Riley," he continued. "When you live in alignment with your soul, you don't just find purpose. You *become* it."

Chapter 10

Oh Captain, My Captain

Elevation 16,476 feet

The wind, once again, played with my tent, pulling at the fabric like an old friend eager to dance. As they tussled, I let go, drifting off into a deep slumber.

The sound of enemy gunfire is all around me. Our unit has been pushed back from our position, but many members of our platoon have been wounded and still lie out there on the battlefield. My captain tells us we have to go back and get them. But I'm afraid. I don't want to die. But I know he's right.

I jump out of the trench where I've been hiding and start running back to the forest where the wounded are. I come to a large hole in the ground, from a shell that has exploded, and at the bottom lies a soldier, bloodied and covered in dirt, but still breathing. I climb down and the soldier turns to look at me. But it's me, or someone who looks like me. The soldier can't speak, but they smile, happy I've come for them.

"Don't worry," I said. "I'm going to get you out of here." My radio crackles to life. It's the captain. He wants me to come right away because he needs help with another soldier. I whisper back into the radio, not wanting the enemy to know my position. "I can't help you, Sir," I say. "I'm already helping someone."

The captain gets angry and orders me to come. Hearing the conversation, the wounded soldier looks at me, wide-eyed and afraid. "Don't worry," I say. "I won't leave you."

Another dream. My cold hands scribbled the details into my journal. It was our third day on the mountain, and each morning seemed to grow colder. Santiago said we'd reach Camp One by early afternoon. I was looking forward to the cook tent and sitting at a table to eat.

The terrain was getting steeper. Sometimes I'd take a step only to slide halfway back down. Around midmorning, we came to a fork in the trail. There was a large stone on the path to the right that was engraved with some writing. When I bent closer to look, I didn't recognize the language. It wasn't Spanish.

"What's this?" I asked.

"It's an ancient signpost, long before our time."

"Do you know what the inscription says?"

"Yes," Santiago replied. "It says it's a sacred way, but only for those invited."

I tried to follow it with my eyes as it wound its way up the mountain.

"Where does it go?"

"To the summit, as does this one." Santiago pointed to the other.

"Yeah, but that one takes us straight into those rock sections that look scary. We'd need ropes for that. The sacred one looks a lot easier."

"It does, but we can't take it. It's not our path."

90

The Call to Climb

"You said it's ancient, so whoever wrote that is long gone. I don't think they'd mind."

"I don't make the rules on the mountain, Riley. All I know is, this is not your path, which means that this other one is."

Santiago and Osvaldo both began climbing up the steeper path on the left. There were times we were on all fours as we scrambled up toward the cliffs. I was sweating so much I had to unzip my jacket.

We stopped on a small ledge to catch our breath and take a drink from the little water we had left.

"Haven't you been up this route before?" I asked Santiago.

"No," he said. "Everyone called to climb has a different path. I don't know the way until we're here. Then it unfolds."

"So you're saying this is my path?" I asked, staring at the rocks ahead.

"Yes, and the marker stone we saw back there—that was someone else's path. We didn't take it because it wasn't meant for you. It's theirs and it deserves to be honored."

"You said that to me yesterday, to 'honor my path.'"

Santiago sat on the edge of the rock, looking out over the valley below. "Honoring your path means respecting who you are. It means recognizing the value of your unique gifts and knowing why you're needed in this world. Riley, the greatest gift you can offer is to be yourself. But that's not always easy, is it? It takes courage, especially when your paths are different from everyone else's. It takes strength to go against the crowd."

I nodded. "I've been thinking a lot about that. I'm more concerned about what people think of me than I care to admit. I don't want to live my life like that anymore."

91

Oh Captain, My Captain

"Exactly," Santiago said. "But honoring your path isn't just about respecting it. It means you walk it—you don't abandon it, even when it gets hard. And if you stray from it, you come back. You stay faithful to the path of your soul."

"I want to," I said.

"When the ego is in charge, your life can easily devolve into those repetitive patterns—the ones driven by your subconscious. This is why you must stay vigilant, living an examined life, not one on autopilot. The poet William Henley was right when he wrote, 'I am the master of my fate, the captain of my soul.'"

"I love that poem," I said.

"If you want a different life, it begins by making different decisions so that you can step into the larger adventure of your soul. This is what it means to honor your path."

We began climbing again and finally reached the thick rock bands that jutted out of the mountain. I thought we'd need ropes but now I could see a path that ascended up a narrow chute. It was like climbing up a giant slide with walls of rock on either side.

"Camp One should be at the top of this chute," said Santiago. "Be careful because the rocks are slippery."

As we worked our way up through this last section, I was slowly beginning to connect the dots from everything Santiago had told me since we met. Things were becoming clearer, as if I was waking from a long sleep. Even the fact that I'd been afraid to lose my job earlier, when it obviously was not aligned with my soul, showed me how much my perspective had changed.

92

The Call to Climb

I didn't want to waste any more time living someone else's life. I wanted to live mine. I didn't want to waste any more days in mindless patterns that served my ego but not my soul. I wanted to live more intentionally. I didn't want to lose another day, worried about what people thought. I wanted to honor my path, and ultimately fulfill my destiny.

Santiago reached the plateau first and waited for me. As I got close, he bent over and extended his hand. I grabbed it as he pulled me up and onto the plateau. There in the middle stood the cook tent, and the luxuries of Camp One. A wave of relief swept over me and I couldn't help but smile. Juan and Luisa, the two young porters, leapt from their folding chairs and waved excitedly as they saw us. For some reason, seeing them jogged my memory of my dream last night. I couldn't help but laugh.

"What's so funny?" Santiago asked.

"I just remembered my dream. I was in a war, and I ran back into the battle to save someone. But the soldier was actually me. Come to think of it, I think it was my soul, dirtied and bloodied, but happy to see me. In my dream I made a promise that I wouldn't abandon them, no matter what other people, including the captain, wanted me to do. Because, as you reminded me today, I am the master of my fate, the captain of my soul."

Santiago put his hand on my shoulder, and his face beamed with pride. "C'mon," he said. "Let's enjoy some great food, and much-needed rest. Then after a recharge here in camp, we'll continue the climb, for the most difficult section of the mountain is still to come."

93

Oh Captain, My Captain

Key Takeaways for Section II

1. **The Power of Patterns:** Life often follows repeating patterns. These patterns are driven by subconscious programs created throughout our lives. Recognizing these patterns is the first step to taking control of your life.

2. **The Role of Awareness:** Living an examined life requires mindfulness and curiosity. By observing our behaviors, emotions, and physical reactions without judgment, we can uncover the subconscious stories that drive our patterns.

3. **Rewriting the Narrative:** Awareness alone isn't enough to create change. To break free from limiting patterns, we must rewrite the subconscious stories or beliefs that drive them and consciously practice new, soul-aligned behaviors.

4. **Finding Purpose:** Your purpose in life is to be the most authentic and honest version of you. This is your gift to the world.

5. **A Spiritual Vision:** Creating a spiritual vision involves getting clear on the person you intend to be and how you will show up in this world.

For more resources from Section II, visit:
www.iwillclimb.com/honoryourpath

Section III

Here There Be Dragons

"The cave you fear to enter holds the treasure you seek."

— *Joseph Campbell*

Chapter 11

The Avalanche

Elevation 17,119 feet

Camp One was a resort compared to the last few nights we'd spent on the mountain. To sit at a table and eat hot food felt like we were being spoiled. The porters, Juan and Luisa, even brought cookies to camp. As we huddled around the small table in the cook tent, everyone was in a good mood—even Osvaldo was talking. While I couldn't understand much, Santiago occasionally translated parts of the conversation that he thought were important or funny.

I didn't feel out of place, though, only a deep sense of gratitude. This small group of people had already done so much for me.

As darkness fell, the porters excused themselves, followed by Osvaldo. Santiago and I lingered at the table, sipping coca tea. The plant was nothing short of miraculous at helping acclimatize our bodies to the altitude.

"So we continue on tomorrow?" I asked.

"Yes," he replied, but his expression darkened as if something weighed heavily on his mind.

He set his mug down and leaned forward. "Riley, the mountain is about to get more difficult—a lot more difficult."

"How so?" I asked.

"Dragons," he said with a faint smile. "The heights grow higher, the cold pierces deeper, and then … the avalanches."

My eyes widened.

"Most people who quit do so just above Camp One."

"Well, I appreciate the warning, but I don't plan on quitting. My legs feel stronger now, and I'm getting used to the idea of climbing."

Santiago's smile deepened, the lines beside his eyes softening. "That's the spirit, Riley. But up here it's not just your body that will be tested—it's your mind, your very essence."

I raised an eyebrow. "What do you mean?"

He leaned back, his face reflecting the glow from the lantern on the table. "You were not summoned here to prove how strong you are, but for a realignment with your soul. That happens on the inside. Remember in the glacier, I told you about the programs that drive much of your life?"

"Yes," I said, my voice quieter now. "That was humbling."

"As you begin to make different decisions, ones that are more in line with your soul, you're going to encounter that resistance we talked about. Heavy resistance."

"I figured. But I think I'm ready … at least I hope so."

"You'll find out soon enough," he said. "But I believe in you."

The optimism I'd felt earlier began to fade, replaced by a quiet unease.

"I want to tell you something important," Santiago said. "Inside every person is a drive to meet three fundamental needs: to feel love and acceptance, to feel strong and capable enough to control their lives, and to know they add value to the world. These needs are universal."

"That makes sense," I said.

"Most of the internal resistance you'll encounter happens when these needs feel threatened. But the solution is already within you."

"So what's the secret?" I asked.

"Your identity," he answered. "The way you see yourself is not merely a reflection in the mirror; it's a lens through which your entire world is filtered. And as you'll see, it's the source of your strength—strength you'll need to restore autonomy over your life."

I was quiet, letting his words sink in. "So I guess the real question is: 'Who am I?'"

"Exactly," Santiago said. "And more importantly, who are you without the masks?"

"What do you mean by masks?" I asked.

"Masks are the roles we play. They're creations of the ego to hide parts of who we are. Early in life, we discover what earns us love and what causes rejection, and so we adapt. Over time, these adaptations become the masks we wear. The more we hide behind them, the more disconnected we become from our true selves."

"So the key is to take off the masks," I said.

Santiago nodded. "And the mountain is pretty good at removing them."

99

The Avalanche

"That sounds ... painful," I said.

"It can be, but think of it this way: every renovation begins with a demolition, an unmasking of what was there before."

"I thought climbing this mountain was about finding myself."

He shook his head. "Who you are isn't something you 'find'—it's something you choose. But this requires a bold act of reclaiming your story. Think of it this way: When you were born, you were a book with blank pages. Over time, your caregivers, society, and your own ego began to write in those pages, layering their ideas of who you are and who you should be. Eventually, you grew up, and someone handed it back to you and said, 'Here you are, this is you, now play the part.' But as that happened, you sensed something was not right, that things didn't quite fit."

He paused to let it sink in. "'Discovering yourself' means having the courage to take the pens back from everybody and decide for yourself what belongs in your story."

I took a deep breath and had another sip of my tea. "I just want to do something great with my life."

"We all do," Santiago said. "But sometimes the first step toward greatness isn't planning or strategizing. Sometimes it's pausing to reconnect with the truth—the truth about yourself."

Santiago stood, zipping up his jacket and putting on his gloves.

"We'll talk more tomorrow when we climb. Just know this: your identity determines your altitude, and your true identity—the one aligned with your soul—has no limits."

As he got to the door, he paused and turned back. "Get a good sleep tonight. I have a feeling we're going to need it."

With that, he disappeared into the night.

Outside, the sky was slightly overcast as the light from the moon tried its best to shine through. Once inside my tent, I slipped off my outer layers and crawled into my sleeping bag. The fabric crunched, stiff from the cold. At least the ground beneath my tent was flat, a subtle luxury I hadn't enjoyed over the last few nights.

As I lay in the dark, I thought about what Santiago had said regarding identity. I hadn't given it much thought before. I was just trying to make a living. I also thought back to our time beneath the glacier and wondered what kind of programs I was running that I wasn't even aware of. How much of my identity was on autopilot? I felt there was so much work to do, but it would have to wait because tomorrow we would climb. As my sleeping bag grew warmer, my eyes grew heavier. I barely heard the wind as it tiptoed softly along the walls of my tent.

The next morning I awoke to the sounds of the camp stirring. The aroma of coffee lured me outside. I stumbled into the cook tent and had a seat, my teeth still chattering.

"Riley!" Santiago said excitedly. "I was just about to get you."

Juan handed me a cup of coffee and then brought me a plate of eggs, beans, and some avocado.

"This smells amazing," I said. "I wish these guys were coming with us."

"Me too," Santiago said. "We'll see them again at Camp Two in a couple of days, which will be as high as they can go. After that, we're on our own."

Just then Osvaldo entered the tent, but without his usual big smile. His energy was different, as if something was on his mind.

101

The Avalanche

Maybe he was just tired. Actually, the more I thought about it, everyone in the tent seemed different—almost anxious, everyone except Santiago, that is.

"Listo?" he asked Osvaldo, who nodded.

"He's ready to go," said Santiago.

"I think I need more sleep," I said, letting out a giant yawn.

"Did the avalanche wake you last night?" he asked.

"No, I didn't even know about it."

"You didn't? It was huge and rumbled like a freight train for almost a minute."

"No, I was out like a light," I said.

"I'm not sure where it was, but I think it was close. The ones that sound like that? Those are the avalanches that don't leave survivors if you're in their path." he said.

We finished up breakfast and then headed back to our tents to gear up. The three of us reconvened outside the cook tent as the sun was coming up. Juan and Luisa were there to say goodbye. But instead of their usual excitement, they looked worried. Juan grabbed both of my shoulders and, looking into my eyes, said gravely, "Buena suerte."

Luisa added, "Vaya con Dios."

I knew that meant, "Go with God," but they had never said this to me before. It made me feel uneasy. *What's waiting for me up the mountain?* I wondered.

As if sensing the tension, Santiago smiled and said, "Vamos!" His calm presence lifted the weight of the moment. He turned to head up the trail, and no sooner had we started than it began to snow.

About an hour later, my feet began to feel cold. I tried curling up my toes as I walked to get the blood moving, but it wasn't helping. We reached the base of a massive cliff, its face rising hundreds of feet above us. There was no way to climb it, so we had to go around.

As we walked along the bottom of the cliff, the slope below us grew steeper until it dropped into a sheer vertical face. We were now on a narrow ledge, maybe seven to ten feet wide, with a cliff above us and one below. It felt like walking on a mountain road without guardrails. Santiago decided we needed to rope together—one misstep here, and you'd surely tumble off the edge.

As the snow continued to fall, the wind began to howl. I cinched my hood tight against my face, but it barely helped. The cold was biting. It was miserable.

Suddenly, Osvaldo stopped and pointed. It was hard to see through the snow, but just ahead our narrow ledge was buried under massive blocks of ice.

"So this is the avalanche we heard last night," Santiago shouted over the wind.

The chunks of ice were enormous, some the size of small cars. They had tumbled down the cliff from above and now blocked our path. Osvaldo unclipped from the rope and went closer to examine the wall of ice. After a moment, he turned back and shook his head.

"That's what I thought," Santiago said grimly. "That whole thing looks unstable. If we tried to scramble over it, there's a good chance we'd all go over the edge with it."

103

The Avalanche

It was a dead end, which meant we'd have to turn back. With the weather growing worse by the minute, my heart sank.

"So what's the plan for—" I began, but Santiago raised his hand to silence me.

"Listen …" he said.

At first I only heard the wind, but then, faintly at first, came a distant rumble. It grew louder and closer. Santiago's eyes shot upward.

"¡Avalancha!" Osvaldo yelled.

High above, another avalanche was barreling down the mountain but we couldn't see it yet. The sound was unmistakable. At any moment, tons of ice and rock would come cascading over the cliff, and if we were in its path, there was nowhere to run.

"Quick, to the wall!" Santiago shouted.

Without thinking, we pressed ourselves against the cliff face, hoping it would shield us. The rumbling grew deafening, and the ground began to shake. My heart pounded in my chest. I was terrified and completely helpless.

"Señor, aquí!" Osvaldo yelled.

He motioned for us to come. At the base of the cliff, there was a crack in the rock. It was barely wide enough to squeeze through. Without hesitation, Osvaldo turned sideways and slipped into the narrow opening. I turned to Santiago, who gave me a nod to follow.

I tried to enter, but I couldn't. The rumbling was now right on top of us.

"Your pack!" Santiago shouted.

I ripped the straps from my shoulders and held it in my hand.

"Hurry, Riley. We've got to go … *now!*"

Santiago pushed me into the crack. My puffy jacket scraped against the walls on either side as I shuffled deeper into the mountain as fast as I could.

And then, suddenly, silence.

For a second, it was eerily calm. Then, with an explosive roar, thousands of pounds of snow, rocks, and ice crashed onto the ledge outside the entrance. The ground shook, and a spray of icy debris exploded into the tiny crack where we were hiding. Ice crystals as fine as dust covered us from head to toe, spraying into my mouth and nose.

"Everyone okay?" Santiago asked.

I was shaken but unhurt, apart from the snow melting down my back and the icy burn in my nostrils.

The entrance of the tiny crack was now sealed by a wall of rock and ice. A tiny sliver of light streamed in, allowing us to see. We were trapped.

"What now?" I asked, my voice trembling. "We're going to have to dig our way out," I said.

"That won't be possible," said Santiago. "If it had only been snow, we could have, but there's thousands of pounds of rocks out there. If we're in here, Riley, it's because we're supposed to be."

I looked around at the narrow fissure we were standing in.

"I sure hope not, because the thing I hate even more than heights are closed spaces."

Santiago looked at me. "Dragons, Riley. I told you last night there were dragons on this mountain. I'd say this is probably where you're going to meet them."

105

The Avalanche

Chapter 12

The Mosaic

Elevation unknown

After shaking off the snow, we pushed deeper into the crack. We had to side shuffle until it widened enough to walk normally. The deeper we went, the more uneasy I felt. The only plus was that the snow and wind from the outside were gone, but with them, any hope of daylight. A few steps farther and the passageway emptied into a tiny space, about the size of my living room back home.

"Where are we?" I asked.

"The lava tubes," Santiago said. "The mountain is littered with them. This was once an ancient volcano, and there's a labyrinth of passageways that run for miles beneath the mountain."

"I hate to be the bearer of bad news," I said, as I scanned the walls with my headlamp, "but this is a dead end. There's no way out of here."

The walls came alive as our headlamps danced up and down while we searched for an exit.

"Do you feel that?" Santiago asked. "It's a breeze, and it's coming from above us."

All three of us looked up.

"There!" he pointed. "Just beyond that gray rock, there's an opening. It's hard to see because it looks like a shadow. That's our way out. But first, we need to get warm. Let's have some tea. I think we can all agree, that was a close call."

Osvaldo pulled off his pack and got out the stove. With a small aluminum pot he collected snow that had blown into the cave from the avalanche.

As Santiago watched him, he said, "How many times can you say you've had avalanche tea before?" Then he laughed as if trying to lighten the mood.

"Yeah, this a first … among a long list of others this week." I said. "Like surviving an avalanche."

Santiago chuckled. "I love your humor, Riley. It always sneaks up on me."

I didn't feel like sitting. I was still revved up.

"We have no idea how long we might be in here, so we need to conserve our water, and our batteries. So unless our headlamps are absolutely necessary, we turn them off." With that, Santiago turned off his lamp, followed by Osvaldo.

"Oh, you mean like right now?" I asked.

I turned off my headlamp, and we were enveloped in darkness save for the tiny ring of blue flames from the camp stove. I felt my anxiety rise, but Santiago and Osvaldo were acting like it was just another day on the mountain. I was still trying to process the fact that we had almost been swept away by an avalanche.

"That was terrifying," I said.

"It certainly got the heart pumping, didn't it?" Santiago smiled.

108

The Call to Climb

As my eyes adjusted to the darkness I could make out Santiago sitting across from me, legs folded, and resting his elbows on his knees.

"Riley," he began. "Do you remember last night we were talking about the power of your identity?"

"Yes, I was thinking about that on the trail. You said that masks begin as adaptations when we're young. It made me think, what choice do we have? When we're little, we're just trying to survive."

"You're right. Your programming isn't your fault, Riley. But once you see it, it becomes your responsibility. It's one of life's great growing pains. And as I mentioned, at first the masks serve us. They help us feel safe in a world that's sometimes big and scary. The problem begins as your soul calls you to something larger. That's when your mask begins to suffocate you, and you're left with a choice—remove the mask, or abandon the soul."

"So how do you take off the mask?" I asked.

"Before you can remove a mask, you first have to see it, and discover what it's hiding, which brings us back to the power of identity. Your identity isn't just a list of values you write down on paper. It's a complex assembly of experiences and beliefs you have about yourself that come together to tell one big story. In this way, you're sort of a mosaic."

"A mosaic? Like in art?" I asked.

Santiago nodded. "Have you ever seen one of those photo mosaics, where from a distance it looks like someone's portrait? But when you step closer you realize that the image is actually made up of thousands of tiny pictures. But as you zoom back out, they all blend together to form the face of the person.

109

The Mosaic

That's what your identity is like—a mosaic of your experiences, beliefs, and stories."

"Stories again? I sense a theme," I said.

"Yes, because we're narrative creatures and we tend to internalize what happens to us. Someone might say, 'I'm an immigrant,' or 'I'm a cancer survivor,' while others might tell you they came from a 'poor family.' These are all stories that mean something to the person—stories that shape their identity."

I tilted my head, intrigued. "So my identity is just a collection of these tiny pictures, these experiences?"

"There's a little more to it, but those pictures play a huge part. But it's not the pictures themselves that define you—it's the meaning you give them. For example, someone might say, 'I'm an introvert, which is why I'm shy and awkward.' Another might think, 'I'm an introvert, which is why I'm great at connecting deeply with others.' Same label, different meanings—and those meanings shape who you think you are."

I sipped my tea, trying to connect the dots. "So, just to be clear, my identity is made up of these tiny picture tiles that I've attached labels to, but these labels can be empowering or limiting?"

Santiago nodded. "Imagine each picture tile has two sides. One side is in vivid color—an empowering belief. The other is in black and white—a limiting belief. The meaning you give your stories and experiences determines which side faces outward."

"So who determines which side is up?" I asked.

"A great question, Riley. Who would you like to make that choice? The ego, who is afraid of rejection? Or you, working in alignment with your soul?"

"I'm definitely going with me on that one," I said.

110

The Call to Climb

"This is the crux of the matter: You have the power to flip those tiles. You get to choose what experiences mean. But it takes awareness and courage because those limiting beliefs often protect deeper fears."

I leaned forward. "Fears like what?"

"The fears of rejection, failure, and feeling useless. These are the mirror image of the three universal needs I told you about last night. Almost all fears that people experience can be traced to at least one of them," he said. "But then, deeper still, there's your dragons ..."

Santiago handed his empty mug back to Osvaldo.

"Dragons are born out of wounds to the soul, and everybody has at least one. They're usually from childhood, or a painful experience in your adult life. They are the deepest and most powerful of all your fears and they wreak havoc on your life. Their claws reach into every part, and instead of fire, they breathe terror and shame."

I shivered as I listened. "So when you said there were dragons waiting for me here, you meant my fears?"

"Yes, the deepest, and the strongest."

"Great, and here we are in a dark, spooky cave," I said sarcastically.

"Just remember, Riley. Your fears are liars and your doubts are thieves. They steal your courage, your dreams, and the world's chance to hear your song. Reclaiming your life always involves facing them. It's the only way."

We sat in silence for a few moments while I digested the conversation. I felt the weight of his words, especially about my fears robbing me of my life. I didn't need anyone to tell me twice about that.

111

The Mosaic

"How do I start flipping those tiles, though?"

Santiago smiled gently. "You start by taking back control of who builds your mosaic. Because you are not what happened to you. You have the power to choose what you believe about yourself."

The cave felt quieter, as if even the air had stilled. I thought about the times I'd let fear rule my decisions and stop me from taking chances. If I'm honest, the doubts I have about myself have kept me living small. "I can choose," I whispered. "I don't have to be the person my fears say I am."

"No, you don't," Santiago said. "And that's where your power lies."

Santiago turned on his headlamp and stood up.

"We need to get moving," he said. "Osvaldo and I are going to climb up there to see if we can find a way out. Once I know what the best path is, we'll come back and get you."

"You're leaving me—alone?" I asked.

"Yes, you'll be fine. There's nothing in here that can harm you. Just don't leave."

Osvaldo pulled a large coil of rope out of his bag and a couple of anchors used for rock climbing. I'd used the same ones in a climbing gym I visited back home.

As they got ready, I felt increasingly anxious. I tried to tell myself it would be okay, but I hated the idea of being stuck here, alone.

"One last thing," Santiago said. "Try not to use your headlamp, to save the battery. The only thing that can hurt you here are your thoughts."

112

The Call to Climb

Santiago and Osvaldo took off their packs and, armed with only two ropes and their headlamps, they scrambled up the wall and out of sight. As they disappeared from view, Santiago's voice echoed back down into the chamber.

"If we're not back in a couple of hours, don't worry, we're still coming back."

The sounds from their climb soon faded into the rock above, and I was alone. I scanned the roof of the chamber again to see if any of the boulders above me looked loose and about to fall.

As I felt the room grow smaller, I tried to slow my breathing. "You're safe, Riley," I said out loud. Then I remembered what Santiago had said about conserving the light. Reluctantly, I reached up and switched off my headlamp.

Darkness swallowed me whole. This wasn't the absence of light—it was a void, complete and infinite. I waved my hand in front of my face, but there was nothing, not even a shadow. Without thinking, I scrambled to turn the lamp back on.

The pale beam flickered to life, revealing the unchanged walls of the cave. "It's just the dark, you big chicken," I muttered, annoyed with myself. I reached up and clicked it off again.

The blackness returned, suffocating and vast.

With nothing to do, my mind went to war with itself. *What if they don't come back? What if I'm stuck here? What if I die and no one ever finds me?* Each thought dragged me further into a spiral of panic.

I reached into my pocket, grasping the smooth goal stone I'd been carrying for so long. Etched onto the surface was "$1,000,000," the goal I'd set for myself years ago. It used to feel

113

The Mosaic

inspiring, a reminder of what I was working toward. But now it felt like a joke. How long had I been carrying this? And I wasn't one dollar closer to reaching it.

I didn't want to admit it but there was a theme of failure in my life. Failed relationships, abandoned goals, jumping from career to career, never sticking with anything. On the outside, people saw me as successful. But I was not. I felt far behind. All my friends owned houses and had retirement savings. Me? That was a pipe dream. As for love, I didn't even want to go back into the dating pool, because who would be attracted to someone like me if they really knew where my life was at?

The dark pressed closer. I wanted to run, to escape this cave, this moment. "I can't do this," I whispered. "I can't stay here." My voice broke the silence, trembling as it echoed back at me.

"Stop it," I said, louder this time. But my words felt hollow, swallowed up by the void.

No wonder I don't meditate, I thought bitterly.

As the minutes dragged on my eyes began to feel heavy. Maybe it was the tea, or maybe I was tired from the fight in my brain. Whatever it was, I leaned back against a smooth stone and drifted off to sleep.

When I woke up I didn't remember where I was and for a moment I panicked until I remembered—the cave, the climb. I turned on my headlamp, and above me I could hear the faint voices of Santiago and Osvaldo on their way back.

Relief swept over me. "Thank goodness," I whispered. I had no idea how long I'd been asleep.

"Riley," Santiago called out from above. "Everything good?"

114

The Call to Climb

"Yes!" I replied, forcing an air of cheerfulness. I wasn't about to admit how close I'd come to unraveling.

Santiago rappelled down first, his face breaking into a warm smile as he landed. "We found a route. It's not easy, but we can do it."

Osvaldo followed, unclipping from the rope and immediately chugging water from his pack.

"How was it down here in the dark?" he asked.

I hesitated. "Honestly? It was hard. It wasn't the darkness—it was being alone with my thoughts. I can be ... pretty brutal with myself."

Santiago looked at me reassuringly. "In the silence we meet the voice we've tried to avoid—the one who knows our secrets. But Riley, your relationship with yourself is the most important one you'll ever have. When you're in harmony with your soul, being alone isn't a punishment—it's a gift. It's time spent with your greatest ally, your confidant, and your closest friend."

I looked at him, unsure whether to believe him but wanting to. He smiled, his warmth cutting through the chill of the cave.

"Are you ready to move?" he asked. "Because you're not going to believe what we found."

115

The Mosaic

Chapter 13

Into the Lair

Elevation unknown

Scaling the walls of the small cavern wasn't easy, but with a little help from Osvaldo, I reached the top and entered the lava tube. It looked just like a tunnel you'd see in the subway, except it was slanted upwards about thirty degrees. It was surreal, like something out of a fantasy movie. After a few hours of climbing in the dark, we reached a small plateau, where we stopped.

"We'll camp here and get some rest," said Santiago. "It's been quite the day."

It bothered me that I didn't know what time it was. My nap earlier hadn't helped. It could have been midnight or three in the afternoon—I had no idea. There was no point in setting up our tents because we were underground and protected from the elements. So camp consisted of three sleeping bags spread out on a rock slab. In the middle was a small space where Osvaldo set up a makeshift kitchen. A single lantern gave us light so we could turn off our headlamps.

As Osvaldo prepared dinner, Santiago walked over and had a seat beside me on the rock.

"You mentioned earlier that it wasn't easy waiting in the dark."

I laughed nervously, something I did when I felt uncomfortable. "Yeah, it wasn't. I got stuck in this death spiral of negativity. It was as if all my past failures were coming up from the depths to haunt me. Actually, it was discouraging because it was all true."

"What was all true?"

"Everything. How many times I've failed, how far behind I am in life. Normally, I'm an optimist. If something doesn't work, I brush it off and try something else. But I think I'm tired. I'm tired of falling short. I'm tired of believing it's going to work and then it doesn't." I stopped and took a deep breath. "I don't know how many more times I can pick myself back up and believe again."

Santiago just listened. Then after a moment he said, "Your greatest journey begins the moment you stop running from yourself and dare to face what's within. It's important to remember, Riley, that you are not your thoughts. But learning to sit with them is an important step toward transformation."

"Yes, a friend of mine once told me that I can be too hard on myself. Sometimes I just get frustrated by the struggle."

After we ate dinner, there wasn't much to do since we were trying to save our batteries. So instead of talking, everyone just got in their sleeping bag and called it a day.

When Osvaldo turned off the lantern, the darkness returned. It was freaky lying in my sleeping bag wondering what animals lived in here. But I hadn't seen anything all day, so I figured we were safe. Soon my fears of bats and rodents faded into the distance as sleep made its way to my body.

I am walking alone in an old-growth forest. The trees are old and massive and their giant trunks rise up into the sky. The ground is soft beneath my feet, and the smell of earth mixed with pine hangs in the air. I enter a clearing where the sun bathes the ground with light. In the middle is a very large stump. I climb up one of the sides to reach the top. It is filled with rings, and I try to count them, but there are too many. I lie down on my back on the stump, which is large enough to hold my entire body. I close my eyes and let my face feel the warmth of the sun. A gentle breeze rustles through the canopy above. It is peaceful. *This is a perfect day,* I think.

I awoke to the sound of a spoon scraping against an aluminum pot. The camp stove hissed as I wiped the sleep from my eyes. Giant shadows moved on the cavern wall as Santiago and Osvaldo moved about. I packed my things before sitting down to enjoy my morning coffee, but I felt an uneasiness in my chest. Something about today felt ... different.

"How long do you think we'll be inside this mountain?" I asked.

Santiago looked up from putting things in his pack. "Hard to say. But the air is thinner and we're still ascending, which is good."

"We don't even know if it's morning," I said.

Santiago smiled faintly. "One place where having a watch might be nice, eh?"

We packed up our gear and continued up the lava tube. The passageway steadily narrowed as we climbed, the walls

119

Into the Lair

closing in as if the mountain was funneling us toward a final destination.

After lunch, the cave narrowed further, forcing us to walk single file. Then the tunnel changed and began to descend for the first time. It didn't feel right to be going down. I tried to keep my breathing steady, but I couldn't shake the feeling that something was waiting for us ahead. The air felt heavier, and my morning anxiety clawed its way back.

"Are you sure this is the way?" I asked.

"Yes, Riley," Santiago said calmly. "Everything will be okay."

I wanted to argue, but there was something about his voice that silenced my doubt.

The passageway rounded a corner, and the tunnel abruptly ended in a wall of rock.

I stared at it in disbelief. "It's a dead end," I said. "I knew this wasn't right."

Osvaldo swept his headlamp across the floor, the beam catching on something near the base of the wall. He crouched, gesturing for Santiago to join him.

"What is it?" I asked, moving closer.

Santiago patted Osvaldo on the back. "Buen trabajo, amigo. Yep, this is the way," he said.

Confused, I looked closer but saw nothing. Then, as I crouched beside them, I saw a tiny gap at the base of the wall—a hole no more than a foot high and two feet wide.

"You gotta be kidding me!" I exclaimed. "It looks like an animal lives in there."

"Can you smell the breeze, though?" asked Santiago. "It's air from the surface. We're close."

120

The Call to Climb

He was right. The air coming through the small hole had a freshness hard to describe. Any other day I wouldn't have picked up on it, but after spending a day and a half underground, it was a stark contrast to what we'd been used to.

Osvaldo removed his pack and then his jacket. He then tied a piece of rope around his ankle before sliding headfirst into the opening.

"He's going to check it out for us," Santiago said.

Soon, Osvaldo's feet disappeared into the hole, and the rope slithered behind him as he wiggled deeper into the passage. My entire body tensed up watching him, terrified he was going to get stuck.

Santiago lay on the cave floor facing the wall, trying to follow his progress. After what seemed like an eternity, Osvaldo shouted something back to us that was completely unintelligible. It sounded as if he was talking through a long plastic tube.

Santiago began pulling the rope. "He's coming out."

Osvaldo emerged, covered from head to toe in dirt. He spoke quickly, gesturing as he explained to Santiago. I couldn't catch every word, but body language told me enough: This wasn't going to be easy.

"The good news is we can get through," Santiago said. "The bad news ... it's tight. Very tight."

"How tight?" I asked.

"Tight enough that you'll have to leave your pack and jacket. Osvaldo will pull them through with the rope. The hardest section is about halfway, where it narrows to the point that you'll need to wiggle."

"Wiggle?" My voice cracked.

121

Into the Lair

Santiago nodded. "Think of it like threading a needle. When the passageway is too narrow, your arms will be pinned to your side and useless. That's when you have to use your shoulders and hips to inch forward. The key is to stay calm and not panic."

I grabbed both sides of my head. "This is insane. There has to be another way."

Santiago just looked at me and shook his head. "We are going to run out of light soon, and we have to keep moving."

I stared at the hole. The thought of getting stuck in there made my chest tighten. "I hate this cave," I muttered.

"It's not the cave you hate," Santiago said softly. "It's what it's asking you to face. Remember, the mountain is not against you, Riley. It's what called you here."

It took at least five minutes for Osvaldo to get through. Then we attached the packs to the rope, and they disappeared into the hole. You could hear them scraping against the walls as he pulled them through.

A moment later, Osvaldo's voice bounced out of the hole, signaling it was time for me to go.

I dropped to my stomach, pressing my face to the cold stone. The opening loomed in front of me like a jagged mouth swallowing the light.

"Nice and slow," Santiago said. "You've got this."

My breath was in my throat. Turning one last time to Santiago, I said, "Well, if there are such things as dragons, this is definitely where they would live."

He smiled and then said, "The good thing about dragons, Riley, once you slay them, untold treasure is yours."

I took a deep breath, exhaled, and pushed myself forward, my elbows tucked tight. The passageway went slightly upward as it bent to the right. Because of that, I couldn't see much further. It didn't look passable.

The further I crawled, the narrower the tunnel became. The sides scraped against my shoulders, eventually forcing my arms to my sides. With no way to pull myself forward or reverse, my only movement came from my toes. I dug them into the dirt for leverage, but each push felt like moving through wet concrete. The rock above grazed my back, and I had to turn my face to the side, my cheek scraping against the ground. I couldn't see where I was going. My breathing grew shallow as I could taste dust in my mouth.

"I can't," I whispered. "I'm going to get stuck." I felt myself beginning to panic.

With each lurch forward, the walls pressed tighter. As if I was sliding down a cone head first, the mountain squeezed my arms tighter into my sides.

At that moment, I realized I couldn't turn around, even if I wanted to. I had no choice. I needed to push again. I took a deep breath, dug in my toes, and pushed.

But the mountain gripped me like a vice. Panicking, I quickly tried to push again, but my toes had no leverage. I tried again, but they kept slipping in the dirt.

"*No!*" I cried.

Adrenaline was coursing through my body. *You're going to die, Riley. You need to get out of here.*

"I'm stuck!" I yelled with everything I had. Sheer terror invaded my bones.

123

Into the Lair

I heard a muffled voice a long way off, but I couldn't understand what it was saying.

"Help me!" I cried.

"*Help!*" I yelled as I hyperventilated.

The mountain pressed down as if it had one knee on my back while its hand forced my face into the dirt.

"*Help me!*" I yelled again.

A panicked voice exploded in my mind. *We're going to die!*

Suddenly the faces of my family and friends flashed before my eyes. I feared I would never see them again.

I tried with all my might to push one last time—but my body didn't budge. I was wedged among millions of tons of rock.

My breathing accelerated as my eyes stared helplessly at the side of the tunnel.

And that's when I heard it.

This is what you deserve, the voice sneered, cold and cutting.

"What?" I whispered, my eyes suddenly snapping to attention.

Fraud, it hissed, the word sinking into me like ice. *If only they knew.*

It was the same voice I'd heard beneath the glacier when I looked into the pool, only it was louder now, colder. Suddenly every disappointment from my life flashed before my eyes: failed businesses, projects abandoned, goals not reached—even my brief but failed marriage. Like a movie sped up, I saw it all in an instant—and felt it all too.

"Shut up," I said, as I tried to push back.

So much talent and you still failed ... still broke. What a waste. it whispered slowly.

"Who are you?" I asked, thinking I was going crazy.

But there was no answer.

The words reflected my deepest insecurities as they slashed at my heart. I choked back the tears. Tears of grief, tears of anger, tears of regret that my life was ending like this.

Then suddenly, as if someone lifted a veil from my eyes, I could see with perfect clarity. My life had been dominated by fear. Fear of what others thought, fear of failing, of making people angry, of letting loved ones down. Around every corner, my life was stained with the compromises I'd made—trading in dreams for the approval of the crowd and pursuing success so that I could hope to feel enough.

And now, in the belly of the whale, the ugliest parts of me had been let out, like a genie escaping from the bottle after a thousand years. With nowhere to run, I was forced to hear what it had always wanted to tell me to my face.

Maybe it was exhaustion, maybe it was defiance, but something rose up within me—a thought: *I've lived my life in fear; I'm sure as hell not dying in it.* I closed my eyes and took a slow, steady breath. The fear was still there, but it no longer controlled me. I surrendered—not to the mountain, not to the voice, but to the truth that this might be my final moment. And in that moment, I found peace. I was stronger than I had ever given myself credit for, even as I let go and prepared to face the end.

125

Into the Lair

Chapter 14

Dragon Slayer

Elevation unknown

In the distance, I heard a muffled voice. It sounded like Santiago, but I couldn't make out what he was saying.

My eyes were still closed as the tunnel squeezed me like a serpent finishing its prey. Then I remembered—wiggle.

When the cave is too tight, he said, "wiggle." Santiago's words came rushing back. "The mountain is not against you."

With my eyes still closed, I moved my right shoulder forward and lifted my left hip. Then, dropping them again as if they were my feet, I did the same on the right side. Each tiny motion was a rebellion, a defiance of the fear that had held me stuck—not just in this tunnel, but in my life.

The rock cut into my back as my cheek scraped along the stone. I inched forward, my body pressed flat to the ground. It was excruciating, but I kept moving. I kept wiggling. Inch by inch, I felt the pressure ease, the walls opening just enough to dig my toes into the dirt. With a determined push, my body lurched forward.

And then, suddenly, I was free.

"Oh, thank God," I gasped.

I continued to shimmy through the tunnel as it began to open up. Looking ahead, I saw Osvaldo's headlamp. When he saw that I was free, he turned off his light so I could see his face. It was covered in dirt, but his smile was evident and it brought me comfort.

I was shaking when I finally pulled myself out of the tunnel on the other side. I'd hoped to see daylight, but the passageway led us into another chamber. My hands were raw, my knees scraped, and my chest felt bruised. I slumped onto a rock, trembling and panting for air.

Santiago emerged moments later, brushing dirt from his clothes. He looked at me, his headlamp catching the streak of blood running down my cheek.

"You're bleeding," he said, pointing to my face.

I reached up and felt the cut. The blood on my hand was bright red under the light of my headlamp.

"Looks like you tangled with a dragon," he said.

"I think so," I said quietly.

"Do you want to talk about it?" he asked.

"I'm not sure," I answered. "I'm still processing what happened."

Osvaldo had a small first aid kit, which he used to clean and bandage my cuts. We couldn't stay here long—not that I wanted to. We had to keep moving.

The passageway widened again as we continued climbing. Wanting to be alone, I trailed behind. My body still felt numb. We finally stopped for some food and drank as little water as possible. We'd been rationing it heavily because we were almost out.

On the surface, we could melt snow, so we didn't pack much, but down here there was nothing. As we ate, Osvaldo pulled a glow stick out of his pack and activated it. It cast a greenish glow on the walls around us. The silence was heavy, broken only by the sounds of us eating.

Finally, I spoke. I told Santiago about my struggle in the tunnel.

"It's hard to put into words," I said. "It was like … my whole life flashed before my eyes, but only the worst parts. The eeriest thing was the voice I heard. It was dark and cruel. It said things I've tried to ignore my whole life, but in there I had no place to run. I honestly thought I was going to die."

Santiago nodded slowly, as if he already understood.

"Dragons," he confirmed. "Like I told you, everyone has them." His voice, calm as always, echoed slightly in the cave. "Most people spend their lives avoiding them—the ego builds masks to hide them—but the mountain forces you to face them."

His words resonated even more after what had just happened.

"There was a man who climbed once," said Santiago." When he was three years old, his mother was battling alcoholism and depression. Each day he tried to make his mother happy, because on those days she didn't drink. When he became an adult and got married, he was hyper-attuned to his wife's emotional state. Anytime she was unhappy, he panicked inside, dropped everything, and tried to cheer her up. He bought her things that the family couldn't afford, and he made sacrifices with his children all for the sake of trying to make her happy.

He didn't make the connection, but his dragon was wreaking havoc on his life."

"So what now?" I asked. "How do I fight them?"

Santiago gave me a knowing smile. "You don't fight dragons with swords. You slay them with courage and truth. The courage to enter their lair, and the truth to expose their lies."

"What do you mean enter their lair?" I asked.

"Dragons are so frightening that people want to avoid them at all cost. Entering their lair means you stop running, and instead take one step toward them, even if it's tiny. For that man, it meant that when his wife was upset, he had to stop rushing to her rescue. He had to endure the anxiety of those moments and let them pass."

All of this talk about dragons fascinated me. I thought again about the voice I heard in the tunnel. It was trying to shame me for not having achieved more success, for not making more money.

We packed up and started climbing again. As we moved, Santiago continued. "Most dragons are rooted in one of the three fears we talked about yesterday. The first type of dragon whispers that you're unworthy of love and acceptance. It tells you that your value is tied to your achievements, and the opinions of others."

"I definitely have low self-worth at times," I said. "As much as that's embarrassing to admit."

He stopped, turning to face me. "Here's the truth: Your worth isn't up for debate. It doesn't go up and down like a stock on the market. There's really no such thing as 'self-worth.'"

"But you said earlier that what I think about myself becomes my reality."

"Yes, it creates your reality, but it's not the truth. The elephant held in place by a tiny ankle chain thinks it can't escape. It's their reality, but it's not the truth. If you have a $100 bill in your pocket and it gets dirty, do you believe it's now worth $80? It doesn't matter what you believe about it. It's worth is unchanged."

"You're talking about currency, and it's backed by the government, so yes, it's true—it doesn't matter what I say."

"That's an excellent point," agreed Santiago. "But the day you came into the world, you were also backed by an authority, but it wasn't the government. Instead, it was the One who formed you with divine hands and breathed life into your soul. Is it any wonder why your parents instantly fell in love with you, and why at that moment they would have given their lives for you? Yet what had you accomplished? Nothing. You didn't even have a dollar to your name."

Even in the dimly lit cave, I could see an intensity in his gaze as he spoke.

"In that moment, you were worthy because you arrived worthy. And nothing you can say or do can lower your intrinsic worth because that was determined a long time ago. This is the radical truth you need to accept."

Santiago turned and began climbing again, then stopped as if he'd forgotten to say something.

"I told you that dragons guard treasure. Well, imagine walking into every room, every situation, knowing you don't need anyone's approval to validate your existence and that the opinions of others have nothing to do with how you feel about yourself. How would that feel?"

I tried to imagine that for a moment. "Free," I finally said. "It would feel . . . freeing."

"Exactly," he said. "And that freedom is your birthright."

As we continued, I thought about the simplicity of what he said. There was such power to it. So much of my life had been one long PR campaign to manage how people thought of me. It was exhausting.

"But Santiago," I said. "Are you saying that everyone is okay as they are?"

"No. The night you arrived at my door, you were not okay as you were. Changes needed to be made, but you were still worthy. Your worth and the path you're on are separate things. Problems happen when you fuse them together. Any dent in your worth is only imagined, because it can't be dented."

As he talked, I thought about my goal stone. Why did I want to make a million dollars so badly? But I knew the answer. It would make me feel successful, something I'd been chasing for years. *But why do I need a dollar amount in my bank account to feel good about myself?* I wondered.

Santiago continued. "The second type of dragon tells you that you have nothing to offer the world—that you're useless, stupid, and nobody needs you."

I hurried to catch up so I could hear everything he was saying.

"Have you ever wondered why no two people in the world have the same fingerprints? Including identical twins?"

"I hadn't thought about it," I said.

"It's a message from the Creator that you're unique to the cosmos—a message that's always at your fingertips. No one else has your exact combination of experiences, passions, and gifts. Your uniqueness is your superpower. And when you bring your full self to the world, you create ripples that touch lives in ways you may never even see."

"I wish I had a recording of this so I could play it back each morning," I said. "I don't want to forget it."

"It must become your new way of thinking, Riley. Your fears want to hide you, and have you play small. But the soul knows better. That's where meaning is found—not in proving your worth, but in sharing your gifts, freely."

Up ahead, Osvaldo had stopped. When we reached him, we saw that the passageway split into three.

"Decision time," said Santiago as he surveyed the passageways. "We need to get it right the first time."

"How do we choose?" I asked.

"The air. Let's hope the breeze we've been following is coming from one of them."

We walked over and looked into the first passageway, but it went downhill. The second went up, but we couldn't feel any airflow.

Just then, my headlamp flickered and went out. I tapped it a few times with my hand, but there was nothing.

"My batteries are dead," I said.

"Okay, you'll climb in the middle from now on, and I'll shine my light in a way that you can see the path."

We checked the third passageway and found the breeze we'd been following.

133

Dragon Slayer

"This is the one," said Santiago.

We continued, but now I was reliant on Santiago's lamp to see where I was going. A couple of times, I bashed my shin on a rock that I'd misjudged.

"What's the third kind of dragon?" I asked.

"The third tells you you're not capable—that you don't have what it takes to face life's challenges, overcome your struggles, or reach your dreams. It makes you feel powerless and overwhelmed so that you get discouraged and quit. It's the voice pointing things out like you're 'too young,' or 'too old,' and that everything you want is on the other side of what you don't have."

"But sometimes I'm *not* strong enough. Before Rick hired me, I interviewed for another job, but I didn't get it—I didn't have the skills. Or when my business failed. Sure, my partner ripped me off, but I was also a terrible salesperson, and no amount of sugarcoating will change that."

"The truth is, you *are* strong, but not because you never fail. The message of the third dragon is that failure is fatal and to be avoided at all costs. If you're not guaranteed success, don't even try. But the key to slaying this dragon isn't perfection, but growth."

Santiago caught up to me so he could see my face while he spoke. "There are two mindsets, Riley. The ego has one, and the soul has the other, but they're very different.

"As I told you, the ego seeks validation, so it avoids anything that might make it look bad. It's scared to try new things because it doesn't want to fail or be rejected. The ego sees

134

The Call to Climb

anything challenging as a threat because it's another opportunity to come up short. And it's deathly afraid of criticism.

"The soul, on the other hand, starts from a different place. It doesn't seek validation, but growth. Challenges are opportunities, not threats to be avoided because failure is part of the process. So the soul loves to try new things, and when it doesn't turn out, like when you don't get the job, it takes the lessons and becomes stronger. The soul isn't afraid to hear the truth because it's already grounded in worth and significance. This is the soul's strength."

"I can see how accepting the first two truths is a key to this third one," I said.

"Yes," Santiago agreed. "When you have the mindset of the soul, it takes the fire away from the dragon." He stopped for a moment to adjust his pack and then continued. "But your strength is more than just your mindset, Riley."

Santiago turned to face me again. "You are so much more than you realize. Your dream in the forest wasn't random—it was meant to remind you of your deep connection to nature and the One who created it all. But the trees that surrounded you weren't just trees. They are your ancestors, standing tall and rooted. You are their seed, the culmination of every struggle and triumph across a thousand generations. Their blood flows through your veins, and their strength lives within you. You don't climb this mountain alone—they are climbing it with you."

I hadn't expected him to say that. I never thought about my ancestors. I had meant to research my genealogy at some point, but I never got around to it.

135

Dragon Slayer

"And finally, the tree rings represent both your history and the power of an integrated life. You've already amassed a rich story of overcoming challenges that you can draw from anytime you need strength."

"What did you mean when you said an 'integrated life'?"

"When you laid on the stump, you tried to count the rings. Each one is a year—a season in the tree's life. Some rings were wide and filled with growth, while others were small. Some years were scorched by fire, others weakened by parasites. But they're all part of the one tree, making it stronger year after year. This represents your life. Some years have been difficult, others scorched with fire, but they're all you."

"The last year has definitely been a scorcher," I said.

"I know," he nodded. "It's already dark enough in here, but I want you to close your eyes for a moment.... Now imagine that you're a bus driver. But this isn't an ordinary school bus because in every seat sits a different year of Riley. In one seat is baby Riley, and another seat has four-year-old Riley, and so on, up until last year."

"This is definitely an interesting bus," I said, amused at the imagery.

"Now look in the rearview mirror at their faces. Each has had a different experience. Some enjoyed happy times, while others survived a fire. Some have trophies, others have wounds, and when you're unintegrated, everyone is trying to meet their own needs, getting out of their seats, grabbing the steering wheel. Some want to protect you from being hurt again, so they avoid risk. Others, like the overachiever in you, push harder, hoping that if you accomplish enough, the pain from the past will disappear. But it doesn't. It just gets louder, and the bus veers off course."

I could feel the emotions well up within me as I imagined the scene, especially the little version of me.

"But, Riley, all of them collectively make up you. To be integrated is to bring the parts together to form one supportive whole, like that tree in the forest. Because within you lies the ability to comfort yourself, to encourage yourself, and to be a source of strength when you need to get back on your feet. You are so much stronger than you give yourself credit for."

I opened my eyes, a strange feeling stirring within me— something I couldn't quite name. The imagery lingered, and with it an unexpected desire: to be more compassionate with myself—to treat myself with the kindness I so often withheld.

"That was amazing," I said.

"If you want to know the real secret to identity, Riley, it's accepting the truth that you're enough as you are, and then taking full responsibility for how you want to show up in this world."

We both stood there for a moment in the dark of the cave. I thought about everything that happened today: the tunnel, meeting my dragons, and now this.

"I am enough," I said and then hesitated. "Well, I want to believe I'm enough."

Santiago smiled. "I know, and you will."

Then, suddenly out of the dark, Osvaldo yelled, "Señor!"

Chapter 15

The Abyss

Elevation unknown

Santiago and I hurried toward Osvaldo. His voice was rarely elevated like it was now. The passageway emptied into a vast room. It was massive, about the size of a high school gymnasium. The beams on our two remaining headlamps barely reached the far wall.

The ceiling above us must have been over fifty feet high. And right in front of us was a large circular pond with a narrow beach all the way around. The water was jet black, and Osvaldo was staring intently into it.

"Thank goodness, water," I said as I walked over to the edge. But Osvaldo held his arm out, blocking me. As I looked closer, I realized this wasn't water. It was a massive black hole. Except for a thin ledge around the edges, the entire floor was taken up by the opening to the abyss. Honestly, it was terrifying, like some portal that went all the way to hell.

"Whoa ..." I breathed.

"It's a lava vent," said Santiago. "When this was an active volcano, it's where the lava receded back into the earth, leaving an empty shaft in its place."

"How far down does it go?" I asked.

As if he understood my question, Osvaldo bent down to pick up a rock and tossed it in. After a moment, we heard a faint *tik* as the rock reached the bottom. Osvaldo looked at us with wide eyes.

The room appeared to be another dead end, so once again, we felt for the wind.

"Above us," I said. "The breeze, but it's stronger now."

Santiago and Osvaldo both followed my gaze upward and studied the ceiling with their headlamps.

"Mira," said Osvaldo as he pointed up at the back wall.

There in the upper corner was a dark opening. It was the only one in the room, so the air must have been coming from there. The only problem was that it was fifty feet off the ground, not counting the black hole that lay beneath it. But I knew what this meant.

"So basically, we're combining my two biggest fears into one special attraction, enclosed spaces *and* heights. You guys really ought to make a brochure and start a guiding business," I said.

Santiago laughed as he took off his pack. "I'm happy to see you can find some humor in this. It's obvious we need to scale that cliff and get to that doorway, but we can't do it today. Everyone's tired. We'll camp here, but we have to turn off the lights. Osvaldo has four or five glow sticks left, so we'll have to use them until we get to the wall tomorrow. But let's move away

140

The Call to Climb

from the edge. We don't need anyone sleepwalking and falling to their death."

It was quiet as we nibbled on nuts and dried fruit. I was exhausted from the emotion of the day. Santiago had shared so much with me that my mind was also tired. I tried to ignore the heaviness on my chest, but I was worried. Were we ever going to get out of here? And how on earth would we make it up that cliff? But all of this would be waiting for me tomorrow. For now, I needed to get some sleep.

I woke up with aches all over my body. I was in the most pain I'd felt the entire expedition. This was our third day underground, and the dark was getting depressing. The glow stick from last night still sat on the rock where we left it, clinging to its final moments of life.

"Where's Osvaldo?" I asked, suddenly realizing he wasn't there.

"He went to set the route. He's putting in anchors for us so that it'll be safe. See, up there on the cliff face."

I looked, but all I saw were tiny green lights.

"He's attached the glow sticks he had left to some of the anchors so you won't be climbing in complete darkness. I think he'll be there another hour."

"It's like this mountain just keeps pushing me out of my comfort zone," I said.

"That's how it works," Santiago said. "The brain loves what is familiar, so it will always return to what it knows. That's why we need to purposely step outside the boundary."

"I'm guessing just because we talked about dragons yesterday it doesn't mean that I've seen the last of them?"

141

The Abyss

"No, but from here, you can start taming them, and they'll begin to shrink, losing their power over you. The more aware you are, the less likely you'll get swept away."

"What do you mean by that?" I asked. "Swept away?"

"Your emotions, Riley. Every time you step out of your comfort zone, whether that's volunteering to give a speech or telling your friend you can't take their puppy for the weekend, there's bound to be a surge of energy that rises up within you. It's reflexive and it happens without you even realizing it. Sometimes you don't even know why—you just get triggered."

"Okay, but what are you supposed to do with it?"

"You unclip from it, just like you would from a rope when you're climbing. Once you do, you're no longer attached, and then you can think more clearly and see what's going on. Have you ever surfed before?"

"I tried it once in Costa Rica. I really sucked at it," I said.

"Have you ever seen a surfer about to catch a wave, and then at the last moment they pull out and let it go?" he asked.

I nodded.

"Think of your emotions like that wave. They rise up from beneath with a powerful surge of energy to transport you, sometimes to places you don't want to go. But the secret to an intentional life is to recognize the wave as it's forming. Then, before it can take you into the beach, you pull out of it and let it roll on without you."

"How do you do that?" I asked.

"You don't identify with it, you don't judge it, and you don't overthink it. Instead of saying, 'I'm angry,' you become the observer, the one bobbing on the surfboard watching the wave roll into the beach. Then you can ask, 'What part of me is feeling anger right now?' That separation from the energy is what gives you the space to hear the answer."

"So that's going to take the feeling away?" I asked.

"No, not always. The energy is still there, but you're letting it move through you. We're so conditioned to react when we have strong emotions or to feel like there's something wrong. Instead, you must learn to sit with them, to tolerate the discomfort while it passes through."

"I could have used this when you guys left me alone in the dark the other day. I was struggling to fight off the negative feelings. They were so strong."

"Simple breathing can help, or you can reach out and touch something in those moments, and let the sensation bring you back to your body. It takes practice, especially if you're not used to doing it, but this is how you take control of your life so that you can make better choices. Because if you're not choosing, guess who is?"

I looked at him, puzzled for a second.

"Remember your dream on the train?" he asked.

"Oh, right. The looping," I answered.

In my mind, I felt the dots connecting. "If I don't learn to pull out of the wave, I'll blindly run the program that's in my subconscious. That's when I'm in danger of living on autopilot, repeating the same patterns."

"Bravo, Riley," said Santiago with a big smile. "If you don't live an examined life, you end up being the passenger. Emotions are not your enemy, but they can be your teacher."

143

The Abyss

Santiago paused for a moment while he put the last of his things in his pack.

"There was a woman who discovered a dragon in her kitchen. Her business was struggling and she was falling behind. Debt collectors were calling daily and the mail was filled with bills she couldn't pay. So she stopped opening the mail. It just piled up on her kitchen counter. Every time she thought of opening it, she was overwhelmed with anxiety, and like a force field, it pushed her away. So instead she fell further behind, damaging her reputation and credit rating, and her dragon grew bigger."

"This hits close to home," I said. "So what happened?"

"She realized she wasn't avoiding the mail, but rather her dragon that was breathing shame. It whispered cruel things like, 'You're a failure,' 'You have no integrity,' and 'What would your parents think?' Avoiding the mail gave her temporary relief, but it was destroying her life. Then one day, armed with the truth that her worth wasn't tied to her credit score, she took a single brave step into the dragon's den. She sat down, picked up just one envelope, and opened it. The dragon appeared immediately, bringing its fear and shame with it. But instead of running, she let the wave of anxiety pass through her. Grounded in her vision of who she wanted to become, she opened her bank account and paid that one bill. It was a small step, but it was the start of reclaiming her life—and of shrinking her dragon."

"That had to have been hard," I said.

"Every fear or insecurity is a mirror, reflecting the parts of yourself that you need to accept, heal, or let go of. What you fear holds the key to your freedom."

We sat in silence for a moment, then Santiago stood up and yelled into the dark, "*Holaaaa!*," startling me as he waved his arms above his head. The cavern suddenly filled with his echo as it bounced off the walls.

"Pretty cool," he said, grinning from ear to ear.

I put my hands beside my mouth and yelled, "*You guys are crazy!*" My voice ricocheted in the dark.

Then from high on the rock wall, a voice answered.

"*Vamos!*"

Santiago smiled and said, "That's our cue."

I followed him, staying as far away from the edge of the black pit as I could. When I reached the wall, I could see the rope and follow it up to the first anchor, which was lit by a glow stick. There were three of them, each maybe thirty feet apart. Between them was nothing but darkness.

Santiago took two short pieces of rope out of his pack. On each end was a carabiner.

"Okay, Riley. These two short lines will keep you attached to the main rope."

"Why do I need two?" I asked.

"Because when you get to the anchor, you have to unclip your line and reclip it on the other side so you can continue climbing. You could do that with only one line, but it's risky because when you cross over the anchor you would not be attached to the rope for that moment, and if you fell, well . . ."

"I see. So this way I'm always connected."

"Yes, which is why you will be safe. Now, see the ledge?" He pointed. I looked, but there was no ledge—more like a few rocks that seemed to stick out farther than others.

145

The Abyss

"You might want to rethink your definition of a ledge," I said.

"The ledge is where you put your feet and just keep moving up the wall. When you get past the third glow stick, Osvaldo said there's a short section that doesn't have much to stand on. There you'll have to use your hands to find a hold or two. That's the only tricky part. But then it gets easier again."

Every part of my body wanted to turn around. But then what? Go back the way we came? At this point, I was getting tired of feeling afraid.

With a deep breath, I stepped onto the rocks and began climbing.

As I gained more altitude, the immensity of the lava vent came into full view. Even though there were only four glow sticks in the room, our eyes had become sensitive enough that it was like someone had turned on the lights.

Below me, a gaping black hole waited to swallow anything that dared come too close.

As I approached the first anchor, I stopped. Trembling, I squeezed open the carabiner on my first line, lifted it off the rope, and transferred it to the other side. It clicked as it closed. Then I did the same with the other. *One down*, I thought.

Then I made the mistake of looking down. The black abyss yawned beneath me, endless and hungry. My breath hitched, and suddenly my body began to betray me. My chest tightened, my legs trembled, and my hands clamped onto the rope in a desperate grip. Panic surged like a wave, washing away every ounce of control I thought I had. I froze, suspended above the void, unable to move as the realization struck: one misstep, and it was over.

Then I remembered what Santiago had said about surfing. I paused and forced a long deep breath, then another. I reached out my palm to touch the wall. It was cool but smooth beneath my hand, grounding me. I felt my body calm back down.

What part of me is feeling afraid? I asked myself.

The answer came easily: I don't want to fall to my death. But as I sat with the fear for a moment longer, I realized there was something deeper beneath it. I didn't want to die without telling my family I loved them. We were not the most expressive bunch, and it weighed on me that I hadn't been more open with my siblings. How silly to let fears stop me from telling people that I loved them.

"Riley," Santiago called up, "are you okay?"

"Yes," I laughed. "Just surfing."

Now that my mind was calm, I remembered the anchors and the double safety lines that attached me to the rope. I was safe. Suddenly I loosened up, and instead of dreading the wall, I began to feel something else—freedom. This was actually fun, way better than some ride at an amusement park.

I made the rest of the climb unhindered, even the section that didn't have much of a foothold. Osvaldo was waiting for me at the top of the ledge. He was smiling and nodding, the universal sign for "Oh yeah, you got this!"

A moment later, Santiago appeared. He'd cleaned the route, collecting all the anchors and glow sticks as he climbed.

"Wow, Riley. You were blazing. What happened to the fear of heights?" He smiled.

147

The Abyss

"That was fun," I said. "But I was hoping this was the exit to the cave." My voice trailed off.

Another dark passageway continued up, but the breeze was even stronger.

"We're close," Santiago said. "I feel it."

It suddenly dawned on us that we hadn't eaten yet today. Sitting around a pile of glow sticks, we enjoyed the luxury of an energy bar.

"There are a couple more things I want to explain to you, Riley," said Santiago between bites. "When you step out of the emotion and become the observer, it gives you a chance to discover what's driving it. Is it an old wound, a false belief, or a fear of some kind? Once you know what it is, you're able to reframe it, put a different label on it."

"Like the picture tiles you talked about, in my mosaic," I said.

"Exactly. You get to flip the tile."

"Remember when you told me about looking after your friend's puppy, even though you didn't want to?" Santiago said.

"Yes, how could I forget? It seems so embarrassing now."

"Don't judge what it is, Riley. It just is," he said. "Somewhere in your past, you came to believe that if people are angry at you, they might turn others against you too. It usually happens in our childhood."

"I think I might know where that came from. In sixth grade, a friend and I got into an argument. It spiraled, and soon they turned the entire class against me. I was ostracized for months, and it was awful."

"That must have been scary, especially at that age. Now, as a sixth grader, your interpretation of that event is certainly one possibility, that when people are angry they might turn others against you too. But looking at it now, as an adult, are there some other possible conclusions we can draw?"

"Yes, for sure," I said. "Kids at that age are cruel sometimes. The rest of the kids weren't really against me; they just didn't want to get picked on themselves."

"Have you ever seen this happen in the workplace?"

"No," I laughed. "Although I have heard of some pretty dysfunctional teams."

"One second, I want to ask Osvaldo what he thinks."

After a moment, Santiago turned back to me. "Osvaldo said that the other kid might have been going through a tough time at home, and he took it out on you."

"That could be a possibility too," I said. It had been a long time since I remembered any of this.

"What I want you to see is that there are at least four other interpretations of that event. You chose the one that offered protection so you wouldn't have to endure that pain again."

He paused for a moment to stuff the wrapper from his energy bar into his pack.

"So my question, Riley, is this: Who created the belief, 'When someone is mad at you, they might turn others against you too?'"

I thought for a moment. "I guess I did."

"Yes. And if you created the belief, then guess what? You are the creator."

149

The Abyss

He looked at me, eyes soft but focused.

"And that's good news because it means you can create a better meaning for yourself. You can flip that tile."

In that moment, it was like everything clicked for me about my identity.

"So when your friend asks you to watch her puppy, and you want to say no but that wave of anxiety rises within you, you can pause and unclip from that feeling. You can look deeper to see what program is running and say, 'Oh, I don't believe that anymore.' That's the moment your life truly begins to feel like your own."

I felt a wave of excitement because I had never known how to do this before.

"And that brings us to the final step in the process of taking back your story, which is—"

"Escucha!" Osvaldo interrupted, turning his ear toward the dark passageway.

We froze, leaning in, our ears straining to catch even the faintest sound.

Drip.

We looked at each other and said in unison, "Water!"

Chapter 16

The Reflecting Pool

Elevation unknown

We got our packs on and began making our way up the passage, only this one was different. The rocks here were huge, more like boulders that we had to weave around. We stopped every minute or so to listen for the dripping sound.

The air was getting colder, so we took a moment to add another layer. I also got out my gloves.

"The temperature drop is a good sign," said Santiago. "So is the dripping."

We picked up the pace, knowing we were racing against time. I was curious now what Santiago wanted to say to me before we were interrupted.

"So far, you've told me not to get caught in the wave but to unclip and observe. Every trigger comes from a belief or fear, and once I see it, I can create a new belief and flip the tile. But what's the third thing?" I asked.

"Stepping into who you're meant to be," he said. "I told you earlier that the brain loves what is familiar. Your patterns are familiar. The Riley who came knocking on my door, that's the one the brain knows. But who you are becoming, even now on this climb, is unfamiliar. Look how you just scaled that cliff face in the dark. Your brain is probably freaking out right now, thinking 'Who is that?'"

Santiago adjusted his snow hat, pulling it down over his ears.

"You have to make the unfamiliar familiar. The new Riley must become more prevalent than the old one."

"That doesn't happen on its own?" I asked.

"Rarely," he said. "It's why we fall back into old habits."

I thought of how many times I tried to change but it never stuck. I couldn't let this be another one of those moments. "So how do I … make the unfamiliar familiar?"

"It starts with having a clear vision, a spiritual one, like we talked about a few days ago. Remember, that's your compass. That's the Riley who has to be infused into your identity. It's like adding a bunch of new picture tiles to your mosaic. Then you must keep the new Riley front and center. You won't do it perfectly, but just keep coming back to your compass. There are no straight lines in growth.

I listened, trying to take it all in.

"By the way, what happened on the wall back there? When I asked, you told me you were surfing," he said.

"Yes, I had this epiphany about one of my fears. Besides falling into that hole, I was afraid I wouldn't get to tell my family that I loved them. Because we never do that," I said.

"But you want to?" he asked.

"Yes, but it felt uncomfortable before. But I don't want to be that person who doesn't express their affection."

152

The Call to Climb

"This is great, Riley, and exactly what I'm talking about. When you journey inward and discover that you've been acting in a certain way, because of a belief or fear, you get to assert who you are. In that moment, you take charge. 'I'm not the kind of person who's afraid to express my affection. I'm the one who expresses love, even if it feels uncomfortable,'" Santiago said with authority.

"I like that," I smiled.

"Until it's second nature, read your spiritual vision every day. You can even look at your calendar each morning and visualize how you want to show up in each of your appointments."

Santiago picked up his pack again and we continued climbing.

"But it's not just about the images in your mind—it's also the words you tell yourself. They need to align with the person you're striving to become. That means it's time for a full remodel, creating new rules about what you allow and what you don't."

"What do you mean by rules?" I asked.

"How you speak to yourself matters. A voice of doubt is one thing. But nasty and mean comments have no place in your life. The next time you catch yourself saying anything negative or derogatory about yourself, you have to put your foot down. Calmly and firmly say, 'We don't talk like that here,' and eventually that kind of rhetoric dies down."

"I can't imagine being free from berating myself. That would be amazing," I said.

"Did you know, the average person criticizes themselves a dozen times a day?"

"Really?" I said. "I thought it would be more."

153

The Reflecting Pool

"That's over four thousand negative comments a year," Santiago said.

"When you put it that way, that's not good."

"The words you say to yourself will have a massive impact on your identity. One of the most powerful things you can do is leverage the power of self-praise."

"Praise myself? About what? Things I've accomplished?"

"Yes, but more importantly, who you are. Behind every accomplishment is something about the person who made it possible."

"I wouldn't even know where to start," I said.

"Because you're not in the habit of looking. Have you praised yourself for having the courage to speak out at the meeting with Rick and the Elders?"

"No, but I should have handled that differently."

"We're not dissecting the details right now. But I like how you found a way to criticize yourself in the middle of something praiseworthy." Santiago grinned.

"Have you praised yourself for having the courage to leave your rental car and walk across the desert? Or for the gritty resolve to survive the cold? Or how you're kind to the porters in base camp?"

Every example Santiago shared I felt a compulsion to counter, or minimize.

"What would happen, Riley, if you said four thousand nice things about yourself in a year that were all true? You have a habit of criticizing yourself, so let's at least create a habit of being nice to yourself at the same time."

This hit me hard. I thought back to the imagery of the bus and all the versions of me in the seats. When I criticized myself, I criticized them. Ouch.

"There was a woman summoned to climb. She was a perfectionist, and always critical. When she got home she set an alarm on her phone that went off three times a day. Each time it did, she stopped what she was doing and found something praiseworthy about herself," Santiago smiled as if remembering her face. "Her confidence and happiness soared."

"See, that's why I need my phone," I joked. "But seriously, I'm going to steal her idea."

"The Ancients were correct when they said, 'Know thyself,' but it's not only facts, but conviction. If I told you your name was Taylor, would that bother you?"

"No." I was a little surprised by his question.

"Why not?" he asked.

"Because I know my name is Riley."

"Exactly. And when you know, and I mean *really* know who you are, then it won't bother you what anyone else thinks."

Without warning, Santiago's headlamp cut out.

Osvaldo, who'd been farther ahead, circled back. We were down to one light and a handful of glow sticks. We walked side by side with Osvaldo in the middle as the dripping noise grew louder. No one said it, but we all knew that Osvaldo's light could go out at any moment, leaving us with a couple of hours of glow sticks. After that, we'd be lost in the dark forever.

A moment later the passageway emptied into a medium-sized room where four tunnels converged. In the center was a

155

The Reflecting Pool

small pool and the source of the dripping noise we'd followed over the last half hour.

"Water," I said, relieved.

Osvaldo's headlamp flickered and we all held our breath. Luckily it came back on.

Santiago spoke, but this time his voice was more commanding. "Riley, we have three passages to explore but only one headlamp. You stay here and wait for us. Osvaldo and I will each take a corridor and hope that one of us finds the way out. I'll take two of the glow sticks and leave one with you. Osvaldo needs to take the other as a backup."

"Okay, no problem," I said.

The urgency of our situation weighed heavy on all of us. Osvaldo took the path on the left, Santiago went to the right and in a matter of minutes I was alone again. But this time it was different. My mind was calm. The walls of the cave glowed a pale green, which reflected on the surface of the pool.

Its dark water drew me toward it. I wanted to know how deep it was. I wanted to know what I would see.

I got down on both knees and with the glow stick in one hand I slowly leaned out far enough so I could see my reflection.

It was the first time I'd seen myself since I stared into the tiny pool beneath the glacier. Although it was still dark, I could see my face staring back at me. It was dirty and scratched. My hair was a tangled mess and the bandage Osvaldo placed on my face was peeling off.

I stared at my reflection. And for the first time in a long time I wasn't critical. I didn't point out a flaw in my face or inspect for new wrinkles. I felt calm. I knew there was still a lot of work to do, but I didn't feel unworthy.

156

The Call to Climb

As I stared into the dark pool, I thought about my dragon. Shaming me for where I was at in life, that I was somehow a failure because of the balance in my bank account. I waited for the voice to speak, almost daring it to, but there was only silence.

"I am worthy as I am," I said, as I stared deeper into the pool.

"I am strong enough to live my life," I continued.

"I have something valuable to offer the world."

I paused. "I am enough," I whispered.

I reached into my pocket and pulled out my goal stone. It now felt like a cheap souvenir that I didn't want. The goal itself wasn't wrong, but my reason for wanting it was. I didn't really want the million, I wanted to remove my shame. I stared at the small square stone in my hand. The "$1,000,000" engraving had almost worn off. "I don't need you anymore," I said.

Then I tossed the stone into the middle of the pool. A *plop* echoed in the chamber and perfectly round ripples spread outward until they gently reached the sides.

From my left, I heard the sound of footsteps quickly approaching. I looked up. It was Osvaldo, running toward me. He stopped on the other side of the pool and then turned to run down the second passage where Santiago had gone.

"Camindante!" he yelled. "Lo encontré, la salida. La Salida."

Osvaldo turned back to look at me. Even in the dimly lit room, I could see his smile. He gave me two thumbs up.

"You found it?" I leapt up.

Just then a darkish figure with glow sticks in each hand ran toward us from the far side of the passageway. I had never seen Santiago run before.

As soon as he reached us, he said excitedly, "Vamos, vamos."

We grabbed our packs and followed Osvaldo up the narrow passageway. A cool breeze cascaded down like water into the cave as we scrambled upward on all fours, fueled by an energy we hadn't felt in days. Around the next bend, I saw it— the unmistakable glow of daylight splashed on the wall above. One last climb over a boulder revealed a small crack leading outside. Blinding light poured into the tiny room. At last we had found the exit.

"No puedo ver," Osvaldo laughed as he shielded his eyes.

"He said he can't see," translated Santiago, while starting to laugh.

I'm not sure why, but the three of us couldn't stop laughing. Maybe it was a release of nervous energy. But we just stayed inside the tiny entrance of the cave for a moment, allowing our eyes to adjust.

Santiago put his hand on my shoulder.

"Wow," he said. "You faced a dragon down there. I hope you're proud of yourself."

I smiled. I was elated, and so happy to have found the exit. We figured that we had been in the cave for three days and now it was time to leave.

For so long, I thought I had to earn my place in the world. That if I wasn't climbing, achieving, proving—I wasn't enough. But now I realized that I don't have to be anybody. I'm enough just because I am. I always have been. I always will be. Even if the world never notices me, if I leave no legacy, and even if I'm forgotten, I'm here now. And that's enough.

The Call to Climb

Key Takeaways from Section III

1. **Identity as a Mosaic:** Our identity is like a mosaic, made up of experiences, beliefs, and stories. Each "tile" of the mosaic carries meaning, and flipping the meaning of these tiles—shifting from limiting beliefs to empowering ones—is a powerful way to redefine how we see ourselves.

2. **The Nature of Dragons:** Dragons symbolize deep fears and wounds that stem from past traumas or insecurities, such as fear of rejection, failure, or inadequacy. Facing these dragons is necessary to unlock the treasure they guard—freedom, strength, and self-acceptance.

3. **Unmasking and Integration:** The masks we wear—roles and personas shaped by fear and ego—disconnect us from our true selves. Integration means bringing together all parts of ourselves, including the wounds and triumphs of our past, to live as a whole and authentic person.

4. **Reclaiming Control Through Awareness:** By observing emotions and beliefs without identifying with them, we gain the clarity to uncover hidden fears and programs driving our behavior. This awareness allows us to consciously choose our responses rather than acting on autopilot.

5. **Anchoring in Worth and Truth:** Our intrinsic worth is nonnegotiable, rooted in our existence rather than in achievements. Reframing self-talk, practicing self-praise, and rejecting harsh self-criticism are key to developing a strong and grounded sense of identity that aligns with the soul.

For more resources from Section III, visit:

www.iwillclimb.com/dragons

Section IV

The Beautiful State

"The soul becomes dyed with the colors of its thoughts."

— *Marcus Aurelius*

Chapter 17

Making the Weather

Elevation 18,473 feet

Seeing the cook tent at Camp Two felt like we'd discovered an oasis in the desert. It was a beautiful day, as if the mountain was rewarding us for our time in the cave. When Luisa and Juan saw us approaching, their jaws dropped. We were covered in dirt. Our hair was caked with mud, and I still had bloodstains on my cheek. It looked like the mountain had just vomited us out of its stomach. We didn't smell good either.

Juan was kind enough to set up my tent while I guzzled water, attempting to rehydrate. Luisa warmed up some water for me so that I could clean up a little. I wanted a mirror to see my cuts, but nobody had one. The best I could do was stare into a dented aluminum pot, which was useless.

As soon as my tent was ready, I crawled in and laid down on my sleeping bag. I grabbed my journal from my pack since I hadn't had a chance to write in it while we were in the cave. I turned to the last page, where I had written:

I will honor my path.

Right below it, I made a second entry:

I am enough as I am.

After putting it away, I tucked myself into my sleeping bag. I was so tired I barely heard the soft rippling of my tent as it danced with the gentle breeze coming off the mountain.

For some reason, I'm climbing alone. I'm not sure where Santiago and Osvaldo are, but my shoulders burn as the straps from my pack cut into them. It's unusually heavy today. As I sit down on a rock to catch my breath, I see someone approaching. It's a child, maybe five or six years old. I can't understand why they're up here.

The child approaches and stops in front of me.

"Looks heavy," they say, pointing at my pack.

"Yes, very," I answer.

"You look tired."

"I am."

The child turns their head to one side as if examining me.

"Why don't you put it down?"

"I can't," I say, although I'm not sure why.

"What's in there?" the child asked.

"Just stuff."

The truth is, I don't know. It's never been this heavy before. Curious, I take off my pack to look inside. It's filled with random objects that make no sense to me. Some of them look very old. This stuff isn't even mine, but I can't just leave it here on the mountain. I look deeper into the pack and notice my sleeping bag and tent are missing. That's not good. Maybe Osvaldo has it, but where is he?

164

The Call to Climb

The child continues to stare at me. There's something about them. They radiate innocence and joy. I feel a twinge of envy as I try to hide my fatigue, but even smiling feels like work, as if it doesn't belong on my face.

"I have to go now," said the child, who then turns and continues along the path, skipping happily as their head bobs from side to side.

I woke up from my nap and made my way back to the cook tent. I still felt exhausted, but it was nice to have some downtime. The camp was quiet. Osvaldo was sleeping, and Juan and Luisa were working to prepare dinner.

Santiago wasn't in his tent, and after a few minutes of searching, I found him sitting on a huge boulder on the edge of camp.

"Riley," he said, "scramble up here. The view is gorgeous."

I made quick work of the rock, which must have been about twelve feet high.

"Whoa," I said. "What a view."

From the boulder, the world stretched out endlessly. Below us, the valley fell away in layers of shadow and light. Miles below, a single river snaked through a valley of rock.

"Look around you, Riley. The mountains, the snow, the rivers—it's all part of something greater, a divine hand that has connected everything."

"I wish I had a camera. This is the nicest day we've had yet," I said.

"Could you feel it today?" Santiago asked. "The energy of the mountain?"

I thought for a moment. "Yes, I could. It was more than just the sunshine. I felt like the mountain was celebrating us. Maybe I was just happy to be out of the cave, but it felt like something more."

165

Making the Weather

"Your senses are waking up, Riley. You're beginning to get back in touch with the things unseen, like energy. When we cut ourselves off from the soul, we begin to disconnect from it. But it's all around us."

"Half of me believes in things like that, while my other half is skeptical. I am definitely a product of my two parents. My father is a pragmatic, science-minded person, while my mother has crystals and does Reiki. And to think they're still married after all these years," I said.

"They sound like a wonderful couple. It's good to use science and data, but it's also good to keep an open mind regarding the things we can't explain. After all, a lot of what we call science today was once regarded as mystical."

We sat for a moment, taking in the view. The expanse before us was mind-blowing.

"Everything is energy, Riley. This mountain, the rock we're sitting on, that glacier over there. There's a reason why the Aboriginal tribes around the world believe that everything in nature has a spirit. Even our thoughts contain energy. Do you remember when we first approached the mountain and it got stormy?"

"Yes." I laughed. "You told me it was a reflection of what was going on inside of me. I thought you were crazy for saying I was controlling the weather."

"And yet you were," Santiago grinned. "In life, we create our weather. Each person gets out of bed in the morning and sets their own forecast for the day. But most have no idea they're doing it."

"Are we talking about actual weather here, or energy?" I asked.

166

The Call to Climb

"Energy," he smiled. "More specifically, energetic states."

"If my dad were here, he'd be rolling his eyes right now." I laughed.

"I'm sure." Santiago smiled. "But even your father would agree that if someone enters a room and they're really angry, you can feel it. Or spend an hour in a small space with a bunch of stressed-out people, and you'll talk about how you can 'cut the tension with a knife.'"

"Oh my goodness, you just reminded me of when Rick got into the rental car to yell at me. Tension! That thing felt like a microwave." I shook my head, reliving the memory. "So when you say 'energetic state,' you just mean their emotions, right?"

"Not just their emotions, but the vibration they're living in. I can't feel your emotions, Riley, only you can. But I can feel your energy, and all energy has a frequency."

I thought for a moment of how I felt around Santiago. His calming presence was hard to describe.

"The important thing to know is that the state of energy you live in will have vast implications for your life. And when it comes to energetic states, there are only two. There is the Beautiful State, and then there's the Turbulent State. There is no third state."

"Beautiful or Turbulent. We've definitely seen both on this climb," I said.

"Exactly. The Beautiful State is characterized by energy from love, joy, gratitude, peace, and connection—it's a state of purpose and presence. In contrast, the Turbulent State is entirely different. It's ruled by worry, fear, anger, and stress—a state of suffering."

"I am definitely familiar with the struggle, especially as of late," I said. "Like the night I showed up at your house."

Santiago chuckled. "Yes, you barely made it inside before the storm hit," he smiled.

"Well, can you blame me? Look at the day I had," I said.

"And this is my point, Riley. Most people go through life living in the chaos of a Turbulent State because they let their circumstances determine how they feel. You get to create the weather. And when you don't, the weather will be created for you."

"Created by whom?" I asked.

"Our programs. When you're not intentional about your life, your programs will choose your state for you. Your state has little to do with your circumstances and everything to do with your focus."

"Little to do with your circumstances?" I asked. "Maybe you haven't experienced the kind of days I've had before," I said, feeling a little defensive.

Santiago nodded. "Life will always bring storms, but the state you live in is your choice. You choose whether a setback is a lesson or a curse, whether pain becomes a teacher or a tormentor. The Beautiful State doesn't ignore suffering—it helps you move through it without losing yourself."

"I have a friend who can always find a way to ruin a good day," I said. "She could win the lottery and she'd find a problem. Sometimes I want to ask her, 'What would it take for you to be happy for an entire day?' But then I never have the guts to ask."

"That's what happens when you let the outside determine the inside," Santiago explained. "When you live in this energy, it's not just negative emotions you feel—it impacts how you see

168

The Call to Climb

life and the decisions you make. Because in a Turbulent State, you see the world through a lens of limitation, and there it's hard to be creative."

"But are you saying I should always be happy? That seems unrealistic."

"No, not at all. Emotions are real and not to be judged. We don't control how they come to us. But, as you learned in the cave, you are not your emotions. If you notice that you are in a state of fear, you now get to choose if you'll stay there. Failing to accomplish an important goal is bound to bring some disappointment, but right alongside it can be gratitude for the opportunity and the lessons learned. Losing a loved one is filled with grief, but only because there was so much love. The important thing is that you get to choose your state, and you want to live in a Beautiful State, no matter what."

"'I will live in a Beautiful State, no matter what.' I like that. I'm going to write that in my journal."

Just then, a voice yelled from the direction of camp. "¡La comida está lista!"

"Time to eat," said Santiago. "I don't know about you, but I'm starving."

169

Making the Weather

Chapter 18

Your Rope Team

Elevation 18,473 feet

The cook tent was filled with boisterous energy. While we ate, we recounted our adventures in the lava tubes for Juan and Luisa. Even though I couldn't understand most of what was being said, the look on their faces was priceless. Every so often they'd look over and high-five me across the table after hearing something I'd done.

After dinner, they pulled out a board game. It was Monopoly, but this version had famous mountains from around the world instead of properties. We had so much fun, laughing, cheating, and trying to knock each other out of the game. I couldn't remember the last time I'd laughed with friends like this. And to think, two weeks earlier I didn't even know these people.

As we played I couldn't help but reflect on my life back home, and the routine I've been stuck in. I'd grind all week, run errands on Saturday, then try to rest up Sunday before the dread of Monday moved in like a storm cloud. I couldn't do that anymore. I made a decision at that moment to have more fun in my life, otherwise why work so hard? What was it all for?

After we cleaned up, everyone went to bed, leaving Santiago and me alone in the cook tent drinking tea.

"That was fun," I said. "It's been a long time."

Santiago smiled. "The soul loves connection. It's moments like these that remind us what's important."

"I was thinking about the last couple of years of my life," I said. "I used to be a person who was always happy and upbeat. But after so many struggles, and disappointments, I'm a lot more cynical now. I can feel it. But I don't want to be that way. How do I make the Beautiful State the norm?" I asked.

"You do this by setting your intention when you start your day. When you wake up, instead of rushing off to work, take time to get quiet, go inward. Revisit your spiritual vision and ask yourself how you want to show up today."

"I have to meditate?" I asked.

"You can, but that's not necessary. The most important thing is to prime your mind. Think about what's good in your life, what you're grateful for, and about the people who are important to you. Make the weather before you leave your house."

"I don't mean to be a cynic, but I can see that lasting a couple of hours until something happens that annoys me. At that point I'm probably going back to a Turbulent State."

"You have to think about it as a habit. It takes time to make your habits but then your habits make you. That's why at the end of the day, before you go to bed, you can do a quick review and ask yourself how it went. Where did you get knocked off balance? What did you learn? What burdens are you carrying?"

"You just reminded me of my dream this afternoon," I said. I told him about the child on the mountain and the pack I was struggling to carry.

"Do you remember any emotions from the dream? Emotions are often a key to understanding them."

"I was tired, but I guess that's not an emotion. I remember feeling sad … even a little embarrassed. This child was bursting with energy and here I was exhausted and complaining about the weight of my pack."

Santiago listened while he put the kettle back on the stove.

"The child in the dream is your soul," he said.

"Really?"

"Yes, the soul's true nature is childlike. And, as I told you last night, it embodies the energy of the Beautiful State; love, joy, gratitude, and connection."

"So the pack is obviously something I'm carrying. Something that's weighing me down." I paused for a moment as I revisited the encounter.

"Yes, but something you didn't realize you were carrying," he said. "And something you've left behind, or neglected."

"Right," I said, "my sleeping bag and tent."

The wind suddenly appeared and sent a ripple along the length of the cook tent.

"Our souls are wired for relationships—without them, we wither."

Santiago took his finger and began to draw imaginary concentric circles on the table. "Relationships are like these rings," he said. "At the center is the smallest circle—the people closest to your soul, your rope team. These are the ones who see you, truly see you, and love you as you are. They're the ones who walk beside you, even in your darkest moments, and celebrate your success. Often your connection with them spans both time and distance."

He pointed to the next imaginary circle. "Here, in the next ring are the companions of your journey—those you share parts of your life with but who may not see the depths of your soul. They're important, but they don't live at your core."

He traced the outer rings. "The further out you go, the more distant the connections. Acquaintances, colleagues, people you meet in passing. These people come and go throughout our journey. Each circle matters, but the energy you give should match the distance from your center."

Santiago looked up, his expression thoughtful. "The challenge is this: to honor each circle while protecting the center. Let the closest ones nurture your soul, and don't waste your energy pulling those from the outer circles into places they don't belong. It's about boundaries."

"This reminds me of a lecture I once attended where the speaker told us to cut everyone out of our life who didn't add to it."

"And what did you think of that?" He asked.

"At the time, it sounded empowering—like taking control of my life and focusing only on what serves me. But now … it feels harsh, almost transactional. Aren't relationships supposed to be about more than just what someone can give you?"

Santiago nodded, a small smile forming. "Exactly. Life isn't a ledger where you measure people by what they add or subtract.

174

The Call to Climb

Relationships are ecosystems—they thrive on balance, reciprocity, and connection. Cutting someone out might bring clarity, but it can also rob you of an opportunity to grow or heal."

He drew another circle on the far right side of the table. "Instead of asking who to cut out, ask what role they play in your life. Are they teaching you patience? Resilience? Discipline? Not every connection is easy, but that doesn't make it worthless. Relationships have a way of triggering us, activating old wounds and even dragons. In this way, they're a fantastic mirror to better understand our inner life."

"But what if the person doesn't respect those boundaries? Or if they keep causing harm?" I asked.

Santiago nodded slowly, as if affirming an unfortunate truth. "Then, of course, there are times you need to step away, to cut the rope. Some relationships aren't meant to continue, especially if they harm your soul."

Santiago returned his finger to the table, retracing the smallest circle in the center. "And that," he said, "brings us back here—the people closest to your soul. These relationships are treasures."

He looked up at me, his gaze steady. "It's easy to think of your inner circle as the people who should always have your back, who'll be there when you're struggling. And they should. But relationships aren't one-sided. You can't be the friend who only takes, who only shows up to dump your problems. You're also a source of strength to them."

I thought for a moment of my inner circle. I'd laid a lot of my burdens on them over the last year, but I didn't do a great job of being there for them.

175

Your Rope Team

"When you refine your spiritual vision, include in it how you want to show up for your relationships, and what boundaries are the most important."

He tapped the center of the circle. "This is your rope team. If these connections are strong, they'll carry you through life's hardest climbs. But that strength comes from the effort you put in as much as the love you receive. It takes courage to have close connections, yet those connections, when healthy, are what it means to live in the Beautiful State."

I sighed deeply. "The things I left behind, in my dream, that might be my inner circle. I want to show up for them more consistently. Appreciate them more, express it more," I said.

Santiago smiled. "We're all a work in progress, Riley. Just remember, when you bring the most authentic version of yourself to this world, and don't let any fears hold you back, you become an inspiration and source of strength for others, especially those on your rope team."

Santiago got up from the table and walked over to the stove to refill his tea. When he returned to the table and sat down, he had a serious look on his face.

"When relationships falter, it can weigh down the soul, especially when we carry the burdens in our heart—anger, grudges, guilt, and shame."

He stopped to add a tiny cube of sugar to his tea.

"When these things are in your heart it's like climbing with rocks in your pack. That's the turbulent state right there."

"Well, I don't hold a lot of grudges, only one—Daryl, that snake of a partner who ruined my business. And who could blame me?"

"Yes, betrayal stings," he said. "But are you still angry?"

"Yeah, I'm still angry," I said, my voice slightly elevated.

"And how long has it been?"

"I don't know, eight months maybe?" I suddenly felt annoyed talking about him. "All I can say is I hope karma is real because I'd love to see Daryl get what he deserves."

The wounds still felt raw from my business falling apart. I used to lie awake for hours in disbelief at how a friend could betray me like that. The entire experience rattled me to my core. It even made me question the loyalty of my other friends. I could still see his stupid face when I confronted him, so smug, so … evil.

"There's an energy in the body that comes from the heart. It's the one you see in children. But the heart can be fragile and when it gets wounded it hardens over."

"Like when someone hurts us?" I asked.

"Yes," he nodded. "And when the heart begins to harden, it no longer radiates with energy. So the question, Riley, is what has wounded your heart?"

For some reason I began to feel uncomfortable. I didn't know what it was, but I just wanted this conversation to end. Back home, I rarely talked about my feelings, and this climb had been an exception. But for some reason his question felt like an intrusion into a part of me that was off limits.

"The greatest tragedy for the heart is when it's turned into a prison," said Santiago.

"Prison? What do you mean?" I asked.

"When people betray us, or wound us, the heart feels pain and sometimes has difficulty letting it go. It can quickly lock the

177

Your Rope Team

offender into a prison cell deep inside the walls of the heart. But the heart was not intended to be a jail."

Santiago paused to sip his tea.

"Over time, the cells fill up and the prisoners create a problem. From time to time they bang their cups on the bars and rise up in protest, triggering their host."

Santiago looked as if he spoke from experience, like something or someone had wounded him in the past also.

"That's pretty deep. I've never heard anyone speak of the heart like that."

"Did you know the original word for 'forgiveness' meant 'to grant a pardon,' or to 'release the prisoners'?"

As soon as I heard him say "forgiveness," I rolled my eyes.

"I knew where this was going," I said. "This is about Daryl."

Just then, Osvaldo peaked his head through the narrow entrance of the tent. "Señor, ha comenzado."

Santiago nodded calmly

"What was that?" I asked.

"He said, 'it has started,' which means it's starting to snow."

"Again?" I sighed.

"Let's go have a look."

We put our jackets back on and walked out into the night. The wind had stopped, and when Santiago turned on his headlamp, big, heavy snowflakes appeared as they drifted down in slow motion. It was beautiful, and peaceful. I felt a smile spread across my face. I even opened my mouth to catch a few.

"Is this going to be a problem?" I asked.

178

The Call to Climb

"It depends how much comes down. Climbing is hard enough, but when you add a heavy snowfall it takes a lot out of you. Which means that we better get some sleep."

I returned to my tent and got into my sleeping bag. I thought more about what Santiago said regarding energy, but what dominated my thoughts most was Daryl, and what he'd done to me. He was definitely a prisoner in my heart, but that's where he belonged. I had no plans of forgiving someone who had caused me so much pain.

Chapter 19

Whiteout

Elevation 18,473 feet

When I awoke, the wind was howling like a freight train. I sat up in my sleeping bag and grabbed the tiny zipper on the side of my tent, which opened up a small window. As I struggled to zip it open, frost from the walls sprinkled down onto my lap. Outside, it was completely white. I couldn't see anything, not even the cook tent, which was only a few feet away.

This isn't good, I thought.

I pulled on my wool pants and then my outer shell. I layered on two more shirts before I put on my jacket. As I zipped open the door, I saw a two-foot wall of snow blocking part of the entrance. I climbed outside as the wind blasted snow in every direction. It was impossible to open my eyes for more than a second. I began to shuffle through the deep snow in the direction I knew the cook tent to be. For a moment, I was afraid I'd miss it and wander off the mountain. But just as I considered turning back, I felt my toe slam into the large rock that was the anchor for one of the ropes. Reaching down, I found the rope and followed it up until the greenish tent came into view.

I walked around to the front, and after digging the zipper out of the snow, I was finally able to open it.

The cook tent was dark and empty as it rattled violently in the wind.

Where is everyone? I wondered. We would normally be eating by now.

Behind me, the zipper buzzed as a blast of wind and snow exploded into the tent. It was Santiago.

"Riley!" he said as snow fell from his wavy black hair. "I didn't expect to see you here."

"I couldn't sleep. What's going on out there? So much for a beautiful state!"

"It's a whiteout," said Santiago. "There's no way we can climb—it's too dangerous. We'll have to hunker down here for a while."

"How long?"

"Hard to say. When the mountain decides to release us. Have a seat. I'll make some coffee."

"I could use some. I didn't sleep well," I said.

"The storm?"

"Well, that, and our conversation from last night," I said. "About letting go of grudges."

"It's never easy, is it?" he said. "But grudges aren't the only thing we hold in our heart. It's also where we store our guilt and hide our shame. Guilt says you did something wrong, while shame whispers, 'You are something wrong.' Carrying guilt up the mountain will exhaust you, but shame," he paused, "shame will crush you because it's the heaviest of all burdens and the lowest frequency of energy that exists."

Santiago walked over to the stove to make coffee, while I sat shivering.

"I hope this whiteout ends soon," I said.

Santiago turned and looked at me for a moment, as if trying to choose his words carefully.

"Well, Riley, I think the weather is in your hands."

"You're joking," I said.

"I've seen it before. If you want to walk in step with your soul, then you have to lay down your burdens, especially those in your heart. Until you do that, I don't think the mountain is going to let us go."

I felt a surge of anger well up inside me. I didn't even know exactly why.

"Are you saying that this storm outside is because I haven't forgiven people?"

Santiago just looked at me calmly, which made me even angrier.

"You know," I continued, "why would I forgive a guy who was supposed to be my friend, who I brought into my business as a favor, and then he betrayed me by stealing my clients and becoming my competitor? And the worst thing? I don't think he feels bad about it."

I could feel my breathing accelerate as my chest began to burn.

"He's a total ass!" I blurted. "And then you tell me that we're stuck in some magical blizzard until I decide to be his friend again." I shook my head in disbelief.

Santiago walked back over to the stove to check on the coffee, and returned with two hot mugs.

"Riley, don't confuse forgiveness with reconciliation. Forgiving someone doesn't mean you will ever be friends again, or even talk to them again. What it means is that you have released them from the jail in your heart so that you can be free."

"Easy for you to say. You're not the one with the destroyed credit rating and loans that I can barely afford to repay."

"The reason you forgive is for your sake," Santiago continued. "Here you are on the side of a mountain in the middle of the Andes, and you're suffering, still triggered by what he did. Meanwhile, he's out there, probably not thinking of you at all."

"Is that supposed to make me feel better?" I quipped.

"I want you to question the cost of keeping him in prison. I want you to see what holding him, and any others, is doing to your life. Your story is larger than what happened to you. So you have to ask yourself, 'Do you want to be free?'"

"Of course I want to be free," I snapped. "But he should pay for what he did."

I took a breath to calm myself down, but I was burning. "If a requirement for climbing is forgiving him, then we should just turn around right now." I sulked.

I looked down at my coffee and watched the steam curl up from its surface, swirling into the air before disappearing.

"Is that what you'd like to do?" he asked. "To return back down?"

"No," I said. "I just … I need some time to think."

Santiago didn't say anything as I got up and went outside. It was blowing even more fiercely now. With almost zero visibility, I had to slide one hand along the wall of the tent until I reached the corner. Then I picked what I thought was the angle to my tent and ventured into the whiteout. After five steps, it still hadn't come into view. I looked back, hoping to reorient myself, but the cook tent was no longer there.

I froze, not wanting to take any more steps in the wrong direction. But I knew it had to be close. *Just a few more steps, Riley,* I thought. And then, sure enough, the bright yellow came into view. The snow had already covered part of the entrance from earlier, but it was light and fluffy and easy to push aside.

Once inside, I took off my outer layers and crawled back into my sleeping bag. I didn't want to think about this anymore, so I closed my eyes and fell asleep.

Chapter 20

The Dungeon Master

Elevation 18,473 feet

I woke up to a dark tent. *How could I have slept all day?* I thought. I must have been really tired. At least I felt calmer. I was so ramped up talking about Daryl that I think I was rude to Santiago.

The good news was that I couldn't hear the wind anymore. I hoped this meant we could continue climbing.

I reached out my hand to touch the wall of the tent. Instead of its usual flexibility, it was firm. I pushed harder, but something was leaning against the tent. I looked up at the roof, and it appeared to be sagging. Sitting up, I tried to push on it too, but it was also solid. *What's going on?* I was confused.

I opened the tent flap and discovered why. In front of me was a solid wall of white snow. My tent was completely buried. Just then, I heard a noise—a scraping sound that was getting closer. I stared at the doorway, waiting. Suddenly, a glove thrust through the wall of snow, as if from a horror movie. It startled me as a stream of light shot into my tent. It was Osvaldo. He'd come to dig me out. It wasn't night after all, and the wind, which I thought had disappeared, was still roaring outside.

My heart sank as I put on my jacket again while Osvaldo finished clearing a hole in my doorway.

"This is insane," I said to him before remembering he didn't speak English.

I grabbed his outstretched hand as he pulled me out of my snowy tomb. The snow had drifted over one side of my tent, leaving it half-buried. Osvaldo wrapped a rope around my waist and clipped a carabiner onto a second rope that I hadn't seen. He motioned for me to follow. It was impossible to see, which made me realize what the rope was for. It ran from my tent all the way to the cook tent, so I could make the journey on my own without wandering off a cliff.

Inside, I stomped my boots to shake off the snow. Santiago was standing by the stove, stirring something that smelled delicious.

"Whoa, that's crazy out there," I said. "I fell asleep, and when I woke up, I was completely buried. I thought it was night."

"Yes, it's fierce." He pointed at the stove. "Quinoa soup, Luisa's specialty. Have a seat."

"Where's Osvaldo? He was just behind me."

"I think he went back to dig out your tent."

"This storm isn't letting up, huh?" I asked sheepishly, since Santiago believed it was because of me.

He didn't say anything as he set my bowl on the table before getting one for himself.

"Listen," I said. "I'm sorry if I snapped earlier. I got really triggered talking about all that stuff, and everything you taught me about surfing and disconnecting from the emotion, it's like I totally forgot it."

188

The Call to Climb

"No apology necessary, Riley. I understand," he said. "It takes practice."

"I hear what you're saying about forgiveness, and I know it's a good idea in most situations. But I just don't agree with you on this one."

Santiago sipped a spoonful of soup and closed his eyes. "Mmm, now that brings comfort to my soul."

I wasn't sure if he heard what I said, and I was about to repeat it when he spoke. "The storm is not going to let up, Riley. The mountain is not going to let you continue unless you open your heart and release the prisoners and everything else weighing you down."

"But no one is weighing me down. I'm fine," I asserted.

"Your soul seems to be saying something else. Remember your dream—the child, the heavy pack, the fatigue in your heart? I told you this climb wouldn't be easy. But you wouldn't have been called if you were not ready."

"When you said it'd be hard, I thought you were talking about the physical part, like getting stuck in a cave."

Santiago shook his head.

We both sat there a moment without saying anything.

"Let me tell you about two people who climbed before you. One was a woman named Sofia. She had endured some terrible things in her life, things so painful she couldn't speak of them. And then there was Omar. He found out his wife had an affair, and it broke his heart. Even though he tried to save the marriage, she decided to leave him for her lover."

"Ouch, that's sad."

"Yes, but in a whiteout, much like today, Sofia finally opened the doors and let everyone out. She wanted to be free. Omar, on the other hand, couldn't do it. It felt wrong to him. He felt it wasn't fair and that he was betraying his values in some way."

"So what happened?" I asked.

"He quit."

"He just turned back?" I asked, surprised.

"Yes. We escorted him off the mountain. It was a sad day for the whole team, but no one is forced to be here."

Santiago looked down at the ground as if reliving it, and he winced.

"And now he has a plaque on the cairn?" I asked.

"Yes, in fact, the one you reached out and held, remember? That was his."

I thought back to that day at the cairn. I remember how cold it felt when I touched it. Suddenly, I was hit by a dose of reality. I was not the first one called to climb. Others had come before me. Some were successful; some were not. It was a reminder that this was real, with a lot at stake. Outside, the wind continued to blow as the walls of the cook tent billowed like the waves of the sea.

"I can relate to Omar," I said. "To forgive Daryl feels unfair, like he gets off scot-free."

"It's not easy when we've suffered at the hand of someone else, especially when they seem to come out unscathed. But tell me, if you ran the universe, what would you like to happen?"

"I'd like him to pay. The way I have. I know it sounds bad, but I want him to suffer the way I did."

190

The Call to Climb

"And if he suffered in that way, would it make it easier to forgive him?"

"I guess so."

"How much would he have to suffer? Let's imagine this for a moment."

"Can I bring in biblical plagues?" I laughed, trying to bring some levity to the moment.

Santiago chuckled. "But seriously, how much would he have to suffer for you to feel like you could forgive him?"

"Hmm, well, I'd like to see his business fail and him being stressed about paying rent. Then show up to my house and tell me he's sorry. I think maybe then I might be able to forgive him."

"What do you think the odds are of that happening?" he asked.

"Probably slim to none." I shrugged.

Santiago nodded in agreement.

"Forgiving others might be the ultimate power move because it's hard and often feels unfair, especially when they're not sorry. We hold on to resentment, thinking it protects us from being hurt again. It's even harder when their actions trigger our deepest wounds—feeling unworthy or powerless. These wounds create pain that keeps us stuck and unable to let go of the offender because, if we're still suffering, we feel they should too."

Santiago's words floored me. I hadn't thought of this before. I did feel powerless over what Daryl did to me, and I questioned my worth as a person afterward.

"I don't know." I shook my head.

191

The Dungeon Master

"Some people need more time before they're ready to forgive, and that's okay. No one can force you. But if you're here on this mountain, it's because your soul knows that you're ready."

Santiago looked at me, still as patient as ever.

"Do you ever plan to be friends with Daryl again?"

"Not happening," I said.

"So he will never know if you forgive him or not?"

"I guess he won't."

"Which means, whichever you do, will have no impact on his life."

"No," I said.

"But it *will* have an impact on *your* life," said Santiago as he looked at me patiently.

"I see the point you're trying to make, but I just can't shake the feeling."

"Feelings can be a powerful tool, an ally at times, but they can also deceive us. Forgiveness doesn't have to be a feeling. Nor do you have to see them again or forget what happened. Sometimes an old memory will resurface, bringing the pain with it. That doesn't mean you haven't forgiven."

I just listened.

"It's about letting them out of your heart with a pardon, meaning they don't owe you anything. Regardless of how unfair it feels, you walk down into the dungeon, grab the key off the hook, and open all the doors. You tell them they're all free to go, they don't owe you anything, and then you just let them leave. And what you'll experience next is profound. You'll feel a huge release of energy that has been trapped inside your heart, waiting to escape. I promise you."

Santiago paused a moment before adding, "Until you do, you'll continue to be a fellow prisoner along with them."

I sighed, knowing he was right. How could I argue? But I still didn't want to let go.

"Isn't it interesting that when people know their time is near, they begin to make amends. That's because they want to die in peace. But shouldn't we also want to live in peace? You have to want to be free more than you want to be in chains."

Santiago leaned closer. "When what's ahead of you is bigger than what's behind, it's easier to let go of the past.

"So how do I do it?" I asked.

"A good exercise is to sit still, and then ask your heart, 'Who's locked up down there? Who do I need to release?' Then sit quietly, and one by one, their faces will appear before you. Some will even surprise you."

"Really?"

"Yes. You might find more people down there than you realized—friends, siblings, parents."

"I don't think my parents are locked up. They're good people, and they did the best they could, knowing what they knew."

"It's not about whether someone is good or not, or whether they were trying their best, or even whether they knew what they were doing. An offense is an offense. You don't need to make an excuse for anyone, you just need to let them go. Sometimes people even discover that God has been locked up too."

"God? In prison? How can you forgive God? He hasn't done anything wrong."

193

The Dungeon Master

"And yet people find they've put Him there."

"I need to go and think," I said, as I stood up from the table.

"One more thing, Riley. It's not just forgiving other people, it's also forgiving yourself and releasing your shame. You learned in the cave who you truly are, so any shame is not yours—it doesn't belong to you. And any guilt you're carrying does nothing to benefit you or the entire universe. It's time to lay it down and be free. The childlike energy you saw in your dream is how you're supposed to feel. You have to trust this is your path, and that you're strong enough to do it. Then simply let it all go."

I gathered my things and said good night to Santiago. It was already dark outside, and I clipped onto the rope that Osvaldo had set up for me. Any footprints in the snow from earlier were now buried, but it didn't matter; the rope brought me straight to my tent.

My heart was heavy, extremely heavy. Once inside, I clipped my headlamp to the roof of my tent and pulled out my journal.

Sitting cross-legged, I opened up the pages and set it on my lap. Then I closed my eyes and tried to clear my mind. The wind outside was the only sound I could hear. After a couple of deep breaths, when my heart felt calm, I asked, "Okay, heart, who do we need to release?"

Instantly, Daryl's face appeared. "Of course," I thought as I rolled my eyes, even though they were closed.

"Can we skip him for now? Let's start with someone a little easier."

I inhaled again, and as I exhaled, my older sister came to my mind. She had bullied me as a child and even convinced me I was adopted and not part of the family. But that was long ago, and I'd forgotten all about that. Yet there she was, standing in my courtroom.

"I release you," I whispered.

I didn't feel anything different. I just sat there in silence for a moment. "Okay, who's next?"

Person after person appeared before me. Some I expected, while others were a complete surprise. I didn't try to think too much about why they were there or what part of me had been violated. As they came before me, like a benevolent judge, I released them.

I thought of my parents. A twinge of guilt plucked at my heart. It felt wrong to forgive them. They were amazing people. Sure, they weren't perfect, but who is? To forgive them would seem ungrateful for all the things they'd done for me.

But Santiago's words came to me: *An offense is an offense.* Even though they tried their best, they passed on programming that wasn't helpful, some of which made my life more difficult. I know it wasn't their fault. But ...

"I release you...." I whispered.

A sense of peace began growing within me as I sat under the glow of my tiny headlamp.

"Okay, Daryl, it's your turn," I said as if he were in the tent with me.

"You hurt me badly. But I know you're not the devil. I don't know why you did it, and I doubt you'll ever see me again.... But tonight ..." The emotion welled up within me, choking out my voice, "tonight ... I release you from my heart."

195

The Dungeon Master

My hand, which had been resting on my chest, pushed out and away from my body as if I were casting him out. Hot tears flowed down my cheeks as I tried to hold them back.

With my eyes still closed, I was standing in front of the prison cell that had held him over the last year. So much pain and anger had come from this place. With him here, I was never free.

But there was still one more prisoner. An inmate who'd done nothing wrong.

The challenges and struggles I'd been through over the last few years had ground me down. I used to be an optimist, always cheery, always trying something new, but I'd become tired. Tired of failing. Tired of fighting. Tired of getting back on my horse only to run into another wall. The truth was that I'd become bitter—bitter at life and bitter with God.

All the emotion from the last few years, which I'd stuffed inside my heart, now started forcing its way to the surface. I tried to resist it, but I couldn't. It welled up within me like water from a geyser racing up from inside the earth.

As it came to the surface, so did a slobbery whisper. "I'm sorry," I said to God.

"And I'm sorry," I said to my soul, the words barely audible as I bit my bottom lip to stop it from quivering.

Waves of emotion swept through my body as I let everything go—my failures, my shortcomings, and the harsh judgments I'd leveled against myself. As the tears flowed, I didn't even bother to wipe them away.

Outside, the blizzard continued to rage, and I, for the first time since I was a child, cried myself to sleep.

196

The Call to Climb

Chapter 21

Three Little Birds

Elevation 18,473 feet

There are mornings when you're jolted awake by your alarm, and then there are those rare mornings when your body gently releases you from the paralysis of sleep.

That's how this morning was. The outside world slowly came into focus as if someone were delicately turning up the volume.

I opened my eyes and felt something I hadn't in years. Peace. But not just a surface-level peace like you might feel after a meditation. This was deep and profound. It was as if there were a lake inside my body, as smooth as glass without a ripple. It felt so good that I didn't want to move. I reached for my journal, opened it to the back page, and scribbled down these words:

I will live in a Beautiful State, no matter what!

As I tucked it away again, I heard a noise outside my tent that seemed out of place. It wasn't the wind or the rumbling of an avalanche; it was ... a steel drum. Someone was playing reggae music. As I listened closer, I could hear laughter in the camp. I got my clothes on and zipped open my door, not sure what to expect.

The sky was a brilliant midnight blue without a cloud in sight. The snow, while blinding, was pristine and pure, covering everything. It took me a moment, but I recognized the tune playing: "Three Little Birds" by Bob Marley.

Singing, "Don't worry about a thing,
'Cause every little thing, gonna be alright."

I hadn't heard music in a couple of weeks. I instantly smiled.

I looked over to the cook tent. Juan and Luisa were having a snowball fight, and Osvaldo was stiffly moving his body to the beat. Dancing was definitely not his thing. Santiago looked on as he held a mug of coffee in his hand.

I walked over, but he didn't hear me approach because of the music.

Rise up this mornin',
Smiled with the risin' sun.

"I had no idea we were having a party," I said over the music.

"Riley!" Santiago turned with a big smile. "Would you look at this day? It's gorgeous," he said.

"I'd say it's beautiful."

Santiago laughed. "Well, beautiful in there," he pointed at my heart, "and beautiful up there," as he looked up at the summit, which now towered just above us.

"They all look happy," I said.

The Call to Climb

"Can you blame them? They've been stuck in their tents for the last two days." He winked to let me know he was teasing.

"Thank you," I said. "For everything."

Santiago smiled and placed his hand on my shoulder. "The mountain knew what it was doing when it called you to climb."

"Osvaldo, though ..." I said. "Did you teach him those dance moves?"

"Ha," he roared. "Welcome to the tribe of the perfectly imperfect."

"I definitely belong here then," I said.

The next thing I knew, a snowball slammed into the side of my head and exploded down my back.

Looking up, I saw Juan and Luisa grinning from ear to ear.

I couldn't help but laugh. This ragtag climbing party had become my family, and I couldn't help but love them as they helped me find my way back to my soul.

Today really was a beautiful day.

Three little birds pitch by my doorstep,
Singing sweet songs of melodies pure and true,
Saying, "This is my message to you-ou-ou."
Singing, "Don't worry about a thing,
'Cause every little thing is gonna be alright."

Key Takeaways from Section IV

1. **Your Energy Shapes Your Life:** Think of your energy as the "weather" you set each day. By shifting your internal state, you can change how you experience and interact with the world around you. A purposeful, positive mindset leads to a better life.

2. **Live in a Beautiful State:** You have two choices when it comes to your energy: a Beautiful State (love, joy, gratitude) or a Turbulent State (fear, stress, anger). Choose to stay in a Beautiful State, and you'll navigate challenges with clarity and grace.

3. **Your Rope Team:** Your soul is wired for connection. Treasure your closest relationships and have strong boundaries to protect your energy.

4. **The Power of Letting Go:** Holding grudges weighs us down. When we forgive, we release people from the prison cell in our heart and free up valuable energy to live in alignment with our soul. This includes forgiving ourselves.

For more resources from Section IV, visit:
www.iwillclimb.com/beautifulstate

Section V

A Mountain to Climb

"Es en la quietud de la escalada donde el alma encuentra su voz."

— *Margie Rodriguez*

Chapter 22

The Worthy Pursuit

Elevation 18,473 feet

We took our time breaking camp. Maybe we were all reluctant to say goodbye. From here on, it would only be the three of us, packing as light as we could to make the high-altitude summit attempt less grueling.

We gathered outside the cook tent to say our goodbyes. Juan and Luisa each gave me a big hug. Juan even looked emotional. Not wanting to prolong the goodbye, Luisa said, "¡Váyanse ahora!" and then shooed us away with her hands like we were cattle.

There were two positive things about being stuck in the whiteout. We had a chance to catch up on sleep, and it gave me a couple of extra days to acclimatize to the extreme altitude. We would need it because the final push to the summit was the steepest yet.

The downside was the piles of snow that now stood in our path. It wasn't so much that we were climbing this mountain as we were digging our way up it.

For most of this climb, I hadn't been able to see the summit. Either it was obscured by clouds or its view was blocked because of the terrain. Now it rose up in front of us, the peak like a massive pyramid of black rock, an impenetrable fortress guarded by sheer cliffs and massive chunks of ice poised to fall at the slightest breeze.

"How on earth do we reach the summit?" I asked.

"From the ridge over on the right side. We're going to head straight up this couloir, but we'll stay to the left to avoid an avalanche. Then, when we get to the top, we'll traverse that icefield over to that saddle in the ridge. Everything from here on is steep, so we'll always be roped together."

"What's a couloir again?" I asked.

"A narrow gully, but the good news is, it looks like there are no more caves."

"You just made my day," I laughed.

The climbing was slow. The altitude made it feel like I was breathing through a straw. Osvaldo had the tough job out front breaking trail. In some places where the snow had drifted, it was waist-deep. After a few hours, I was hit by a thought: Once we reach the summit, it will be time to go home.

We were nearing twenty thousand feet and there was no flat place to stop and eat lunch. So we did the best we could by digging our crampons into the snow, along with our ice axes, to keep from sliding down the mountain. The sun was still shining, and it was warm enough that I needed to unzip my jacket.

"I'm a little nervous about heading back," I confessed. "I've been so focused on the climb that I almost forgot I have a life back home."

"I guess you'll have some decisions to make when you return," said Santiago.

204

The Call to Climb

"Well, Rick is going to fire me, which is actually great. I can't believe I was worried about losing that job. I've also been thinking about reviving my business or starting something new. I know I blame Daryl for destroying our last one, but the truth is, we were floundering, and part of that was my fault. I was supposed to bring in new clients, but I let my fears of rejection get in the way and avoided picking up the phone to make sales calls. I think Daryl saw the writing on the wall before I did and looked for an exit."

As I shared about my business and Daryl, I noticed I was completely at peace. It was amazing. I wasn't angry with him anymore, and I wasn't mad at myself either.

"I've been thinking about our conversation farther down the mountain, about purpose. I'm still a little confused."

"Which part?" he asked.

"You said something else, about a pursuit of some kind, because I'm still wondering what I should be doing with my life. You promised we'd talk about it farther up the mountain."

"Yes, Riley. You need a mountain to climb—a worthy pursuit. Your purpose is to bring your true self to the world, but your worthy pursuit is where you'll find meaning. It's something that's worth your time and energy, something that excites you and aligns with your soul. By doing it, you not only fulfill yourself but also bless others. It can be part of your job or simply something you love doing in your free time—it's the work that makes your soul come alive."

"That's what I'm looking for, but how do I find it?" I asked.

Santiago stood back up and tightened the straps on his pack. "Discovering a worthy pursuit isn't about receiving a grand revelation or a sign from the heavens. Your soul has already left a trail of breadcrumbs for you. They're in your memories, your experiences, your passions—sometimes, even your pain."

"What do you mean by breadcrumbs?"

"The things that light you up, that energize your soul—those are clues to your design. Many of these breadcrumbs date back to childhood."

"Really?" I asked, skeptical again.

"Yes, I'll show you. Think about one of the best days of your life as a child. What were you doing?"

I thought for a moment. "I think some of the days I spent hanging out with my friends, laughing, riding our bikes—you know, typical kids' stuff."

"Yes, but I need a specific day," he pressed. "Tell me what you were doing. I'll ask Osvaldo to do the same."

Santiago and Osvaldo went back and forth for a minute. It was the most words I'd heard Osvaldo speak since meeting him. I had a lot of great memories as a kid, and there were a couple I could choose from.

"Osvaldo told me about a particular day when he was a teenager. His father was in the volunteer fire department in his village, and there was a big fire. The entire night, while his dad and others fought the blaze, he was running around behind the scenes making sure everyone had what they needed. They battled the fire long into the night, and Osvaldo stayed up the entire time to support them. Once they had the fire under control, his mother made him come home to get some sleep. He says he remembers lying in bed that night thinking it was the happiest day of his life."

"That's a great memory, Osvaldo," I said to him. He was grinning ear to ear with pride.

"Look at him today," Santiago said. "Osvaldo isn't a fireman, but most of his work involves serving others behind the scenes. That day was a breadcrumb—a hint of who he was and what brought him to life."

Santiago gave Osvaldo a nod and we began climbing once again.

"Okay, let me try. One of my best memories growing up was the day I rented a video camera. My friends and I made a movie. It was a spinoff of Batman, and I was the director." I smiled as the memories of old friends and simpler times came to my mind.

Santiago chuckled. "And did you pursue filmmaking?"

"I wanted to. But I was from a small town, and my parents said it wasn't practical. So I ended up studying psychology. Does this mean I missed my calling?"

"Not at all," he said. "Your soul can find expression through countless careers. Think of them as vehicles through which your soul can fulfill its destiny. Your natural gifts and talents are also breadcrumbs. The things that come easy to you, that are hard for others. We often overlook them because they feel so natural to us. There are clues even in your desires. Why are you drawn to certain things and not to others? Why do certain careers or activities light you up?

"You can also find breadcrumbs in pain," he continued. "There are things that break your heart more than others, and things that make you angry that others seem to tolerate."

"Interesting," I said. "Like when one of your values getting crossed."

"Yes, exactly. There was a woman who climbed who was a teacher. She loved her students, but something always felt off about the system she worked in. What really broke her heart was seeing kids who fell through the cracks—bright, capable children who struggled simply because they didn't fit into the traditional way of learning. It made her angry, too, that these kids were labeled as 'problematic' when, in fact, they were just misunderstood. She didn't quit her job, but she started an after-school program where she could teach in a different way, focused on individualized learning. Her anger and pain were breadcrumbs, showing her where she was meant to make a difference."

We stopped briefly to adjust our layers. I had learned how dangerous it was to sweat while climbing, so we were constantly adding or subtracting clothes.

"Sometimes I have ideas, but then I think they're not very significant and wouldn't make that big a difference compared to what others are doing."

"How are you defining significance? There was a man who came here a few years ago. He worked in finance, a career he thought was stable and respectable, but it drained him. He felt an emptiness he couldn't explain. As he climbed, he told me about his childhood, how he used to love drawing and painting but gave it up because there was no money in it. His breadcrumbs were right there—from the joy he found in creating as a child, to the occasional sketching he did in meetings when he was stressed. After the climb, he started painting again, and it changed everything."

"I thought living a life of purpose meant that you're making a difference in the world, not rediscovering a lost hobby."

"As he returned to something that nourished his soul, he became happier. This in turn made him a better coworker and leader. He made more space to be himself, which gave others permission to be themselves. Returning to painting helped him unlock other parts of him that he'd hidden that were gifts to the world. The soul reveals more layers as you grow throughout your life."

"That's honestly refreshing. It takes some of the pressure away trying to find a purpose that changes the world. Something worthy," I said.

"What makes a pursuit worthy is that it's yours," he said.

"I like helping people, but I guess that's pretty broad."

"It's a great start," Santiago encouraged. "But think deeper—how do you like helping? Osvaldo serves others behind the scenes. Do you resonate with that?"

"No, I don't think in that way. You said, 'When the path is right, the energy is there.' It made me think of the time I started a podcast. I was interviewing people about how they overcame difficult things in their lives. It was just a side hobby, but I loved it! It made me feel alive, drawing out their stories and then posting them online for others to hear. I didn't even get paid to do it. I just loved it."

"I can see your face light up even now as you tell me. Why did you stop?" asked Santiago.

"That was before my business failed, and I had to find a job. It was a discouraging time for me, and I just left it."

"Isn't it interesting that one of your best days in life was creating stories with your friends, and one of your favorite recent experiences was drawing out stories from others? And even though you didn't go to film school, you were drawn to study psychology, which teaches how humans grow and develop. I can see some themes there. You should keep tugging on those threads."

"I will," I said as the pieces were slowly coming together for me. "I never thought about it this way."

"Most people don't," Santiago said. "They get caught up in what they should do and forget to pay attention to who they already are. That's why you feel drained in your current job—it's not aligned with your soul."

"Yeah, that job is killing me," I admitted. "I feel like I'm wasting away there."

"There's one thing that's universal about the soul—not just yours, but everyone's. The soul, regardless of what it seeks, will never express hate. The architecture of every soul is love and connection. Any desire or destiny that violates these is not from the soul, but the ego. Your soul always points toward what's true and what's authentic."

"I've struggled for so long, wondering what I should do with my life, and each year as I get older, I feel like I'm running out of time. But this helps me see that I don't have to find that 'one thing.'"

"Riley, you could do a thousand different things that are in alignment with your soul."

"That almost feels overwhelming," I said.

"On the contrary, that's the richness of life. Don't stress about which mountain to climb, just choose one that allows you to be in alignment with your soul and give yourself to it. And when you've had enough of that mountain, there are a

210

The Call to Climb

thousand more. Don't worry about finding the right dance—just focus on playing your song. When the path is right, you'll find the energy will be there also."

I nodded as I listened to what he said.

"But for today," he continued, "you're right where you're supposed to be."

We climbed in silence the rest of the afternoon. The altitude made even the simplest of conversations difficult. Eventually the terrain leveled out just enough that we could pitch our tents.

"We'll sleep here tonight and tomorrow aim for High Camp. It's a monster of a day to reach it, but I think we can."

Osvaldo placed long metal ice anchors into the snow above each of our tents so that we could tie a rope to them. The last thing we needed was one of the tents tumbling down thousands of feet in the dark.

"Wow, we are getting close," I said.

"Yes, High Camp is the last one before the summit."

Just as the sun was setting, the clouds moved in. At first, I was worried about another storm, but the evening was calm. All of us were exhausted, so instead of our usual conversation, everyone retired to their tents.

For the first time, I was excited to get home. The more I thought about it, the more I wondered why I was going into work just to get fired. I wasn't going to give Rick that satisfaction. It was time to move on officially. I tried to brainstorm my next career move, but after two ideas, I had already drifted off to sleep.

211

The Worthy Pursuit

Chapter 23

One Thousand Steps

Elevation 20,017 feet

I woke up with a splitting headache and nausea. As I lay in my sleeping bag, I checked my pulse—it was 101. My heart was working overtime just to get oxygen to my body. The air was thinner here, sharper, as if the mountain itself was demanding more from me. Osvaldo couldn't get the stove to light, so breakfast was semi-frozen eggs that Juan had boiled for us in Camp Two before we left.

The clouds from last night still covered the sky, and the temperature showed no signs of rising. I was feeling yesterday's push up the couloir and found myself fighting for every inch the mountain would give me. The route to High Camp was a beast—a seemingly endless grind up a steep ridge. There was no fun way to frame it; it was a slog.

We were still roped together, and I was in the third position. I tried to keep up, but my feet were dragging. Numerous times I fell behind, and the rope between Santiago and me would tighten, halting him in his tracks.

After the third time, he turned and walked back down toward me. "How are you doing?" he asked.

213

I shook my head. "I don't know," I admitted. "It's like everything in me wants to stop. I keep thinking, 'Why am I doing this?'"

Santiago looked down the mountain to the valley below. "You've come a long way since you first showed up at my door," he said. "I've seen a shift in you, one that's real, that's deep."

"That's nice to hear. I feel free after the whiteout, and being in the cave completely changed how I see myself. Now I just need to put everything together when I get back home."

"Do you remember what I told you in base camp, right before you set foot on the mountain?" he asked.

"Yes, 'one more step.' I think that's how you phrased it."

"We can be aligned with our soul, and even passionate about a worthy pursuit, but there are still moments when that's not enough," he said. "At some point, everyone considers packing it in."

"I've definitely thought about it today," I confessed. "So what's the secret?"

"Pain management," Santiago said as he smiled. "When we can't manage the discomfort, it eventually leads us to lose heart. That's when we cross the quitting line, when we've stopped believing we can."

"The quitting line?"

"That moment you say, 'That's it, I'm done.' But as you get stronger, the quitting line moves."

"I feel like my quitting line is right about there," I said, pointing my ice axe a few feet beyond where Santiago stood.

He smiled wide. "Well then, we better move it because you're going to cross that in ten more steps."

Calling me on my bluff, he turned and continued up the mountain. As I followed, I thought about my own history.

214

The Call to Climb

It was a mix, to be honest. There were some things I'd persevered through for years, and others where I gave up quickly. I hadn't given much thought to the difference.

"So how does a person move the quitting line?" I asked.

"Remember, Riley, the brain is a gymnast. When you're in pain, it has the computing power to reason its way out of anything. It will offer up the most profound and compelling reasons why it's okay to stop."

"I've heard those voices today, making the case for why we don't need to go all the way up to the summit. They were pretty logical, if I'm honest," I said.

"You just have to expect that your brain is going to do it. As soon as discomfort shows up, the justifications come knocking, and they only have one goal—stop the pain. So the first thing you want to do is change your relationship with it, with pain and discomfort."

"How do I do that?" I asked.

"Remind yourself that the pain is temporary and necessary."

"Necessary?" I asked.

"Yes. You can't build strength without enduring some discomfort, whether that's in the gym or in the office working on a big project. So when you feel like quitting, know that you've entered a growth zone. This is an opportunity to get stronger, but if you bail out, you lose the growth."

Santiago could see I was falling behind again, so he stopped.

"When you reframe what pain and discomfort mean, it gives it purpose. Remember that resilience and grit are like muscles. They get stronger by exercising. If you consistently do hard things—things you don't want to do—it actually increases the

215

One Thousand Steps

size of a very special part in your brain, which in turn makes hard things easier," he said.

"Really?" I asked. "That's one piece of good news because right now my lungs are on fire and so are my legs."

"The other thing to remember is that your pain is temporary. Your body doesn't know that, so you have to remind it that this will pass."

We finally stopped for lunch. My body devoured the calories. Everything at high altitude took more work. Even tying your shoelaces took your breath away. As the pain in my lungs subsided, I thought about Santiago's comment earlier.

"You said pain was temporary, and it just made me think. Imagine had I quit an hour ago when I was hurting. I'd be kicking myself by the time I got to the bottom."

Santiago nodded. "There's always a bill to pay," he said. "Either now on the mountain or later back in base camp, but the one down there is usually ten times the price."

"I can imagine," I said.

"Discomfort, like fear, is a teacher," said Santiago, as he continued where we'd left off. "When you feel like quitting, ask yourself, 'What part of me wants to quit?'"

"This sounds like the surfing lesson you taught me back in the cave," I said.

"Exactly. Because you might discover that behind the pain is something else. Sometimes it's a fear of failing, or maybe you're overwhelmed because you lack clarity. Perhaps you're discouraged because you don't think you can do it. When you can unclip and stand back, you'll see your situation more clearly. Then you will know what you need."

216

The Call to Climb

"What do you mean, 'I'll know what I need?'" I asked.

"Think of yourself like a doctor helping a patient diagnose their pain. When you know why it's hurting you're able to better prescribe the remedy. Maybe you forgot why you're doing it and you need to reconnect to the purpose. When your *why* is big enough, it helps fuel your *how*. I told you earlier that the soul doesn't mind pain if it has purpose. Without purpose, it's just suffering."

"Got it," I said.

"If you're overwhelmed, get clarity on your next step, and when you feel the task is too much, you have to shorten your target into something believable."

"Like 'one more step,'" I said.

"Exactly. If you've stopped believing you're capable, you need a renewal of faith. Sometimes that's a reminder of what you've accomplished in the past. Other times its borrowing belief from a friend. Strength can even be found in mantras like 'One more step,' or simply, 'Keep climbing,' which I've heard you say several times on this mountain."

"Huh," I said, surprised. "I guess I have said that a lot."

We finished up our lunch and continued on. Even the short break did wonders for my mood.

Santiago continued. "Life is filled with days like today, where the goal of reaching camp pushes you to your limit. But there's another kind of strength that's needed, and that's for the long climb. While some people quit a task, others will abandon a journey. Remember when I told you in the cave that you have to make the unfamiliar familiar?"

"Yes," I said.

217

One Thousand Steps

"Your future will be defined by the habits you're creating now, but habits take time and distance, just like climbing this mountain. It will take us around forty thousand vertical steps to reach the summit. The problem is that each of those steps is tiny, so we tend to devalue them. Yet it's the sum total of all forty thousand that gets us to the summit. And if you miss just one, you fall short."

"I hadn't thought about it like that before," I said.

"Consistency, Riley, in the mundane. It's one of the most difficult things for people to do because they find it hard to delay the reward. You must learn to love the process and remember the Law of a Thousand Steps. When you can take tiny steps consistently, without stopping, you can do anything. That's how you grow the business, write the book, or get the degree. It's the long climb."

He paused for a moment to let me catch up.

I felt a gut punch as I thought of all the ideas I'd tried, only to abandon them ninety days later. It might be my biggest area of weakness.

"I'm guilty as charged on this one," I said.

"Everything we talked about on this climb takes work, Riley. If you want to make the unfamiliar familiar and create new habits, you have to commit to living with intention—daily. You have to put in the thousand steps."

Santiago stopped a moment and looked out over the valley. "If you only hear me say one thing about resilience and grit, hear this: The most important thing is your faith—faith in yourself. There's nothing more important than believing you can do it, because that produces hope, and when you have hope, you keep climbing. It's another reason why you need a good rope team. Because, as I said, sometimes you need to borrow a little faith from your friends."

After he said it, I was reminded of a conversation my grandmother had with me when I was little. It was about faith, hope, and perseverance. She told me that hope was like oxygen; as long as you had some, you could keep fighting. Her memory suddenly gave me strength.

Santiago continued. "When you think about it, there are two versions of Riley on this mountain. There's one Riley who's going to bail out and quit, and another Riley who's going to sleep in High Camp tonight. Now, what's the difference between them?"

I thought for a moment. "The Riley who makes it to High Camp has reframed pain, and found ways to keep believing."

"Yes," he said. "We better keep going because we'll soon be losing daylight. High Camp is a quick turnaround so the sooner we're there, the more rest we can have."

We continued for another hour in silence. Everyone seemed to be focused on just taking the next step. I tried to remember everything Santiago had told me that day about pain management. It was the perfect day to practice.

"Look, Riley," Santiago pointed up the mountain. "The saddle. That's where we're setting up High Camp. Maybe twenty minutes more."

"Thank goodness," I said. "That was not easy."

"No, it certainly wasn't," he answered.

The terrain began to flatten a bit and we were able to unclip from the rope and walk on our own.

"Have you ever been to a spa?" asked Santiago.

"Yes, once when our company stayed at a resort for some meetings," I said. "Are you telling me there's a Jacuzzi at High Camp?" I smiled.

"Not quite," he laughed. "But how did you feel after?" he asked.

"The spa? Amazing, like I was a new person. I was so relaxed."

"And how did you feel when you saw your reflection in the pool, down in the cave—dirty hair, cuts, and all?"

I thought back to that moment, and a huge grin spread across my face. "I felt like a badass," I said.

"What does that tell you about life? About you?"

I thought for a moment. "There's something in the climb," I said. "In the struggle. That I relish the challenge."

He nodded. "Don't get me wrong; there's a time for the spa, but you were born to climb. We all were, and it's into the headwind that sharpens us to be our very best. So don't pray for an easy life; pray for the strength and the courage to bring your full self to this one. After all, life is about the climb, not the destination."

Key Takeaways from Section V

1. **A Worthy Pursuit:** Your purpose is about bringing your authentic self to the world. A worthy pursuit is how you express that purpose—a meaningful endeavor that excites you, serves others, and gives your life direction.

2. **Follow the Breadcrumbs:** Look to your past for clues— your happiest memories, passions, and even painful experiences. These breadcrumbs are hints from your soul about what energizes and fulfills you.

3. **Keep Climbing:** Resilience is like a muscle that gets stronger as we use it. Changing your relationship with discomfort can lead to massive growth.

4. **The Long Climb:** Major achievements are the sum of small, consistent steps. The "Law of a Thousand Steps" reminds us that daily habits and perseverance lead to long-term success.

5. **Your Rope Team:** Everyone needs a few people to climb with. Relationships give us courage and strength. The soul craves connection.

For more resources from Section V, visit:
www.iwillclimb.com/keepclimbing

Chapter 24

High Camp

Elevation 21,032 feet

We reached the saddle of the ridge, but it was too windy to set up camp. With night quickly falling, we opted to climb back down and pitch our tents below an outcropping of rocks that provided some shelter. The snow wasn't as deep there either.

In the center of our three tents, Osvaldo set up his kitchen and was able to get the stove working. Santiago and I sculpted our own versions of lawn chairs out of the snow and sat in them, while the lantern brought light to our little camp.

"I miss Juan and Luisa already," I said, rubbing my hands together for warmth.

"I miss beating all of you at Monopoly," said Santiago, laughing. "That was too much fun."

"I can't believe we made it to High Camp," I said.

"One final push to the summit, Riley. From here it's about five hours along an exposed ridge to reach the top."

"How will I explain any of this to people back home?" I asked.

223

"You probably can't," he said. "Not without them thinking you're crazy."

It didn't take Osvaldo long to warm up the leftover stew that Juan had made. Above twenty thousand feet, everything boils at a lower temperature.

"This altitude and the snow today almost killed me. I don't know how you do it," I said to Santiago. "How old are you, anyway?"

He laughed. "Old enough not to answer that, but young enough to keep climbing."

It was another one of Santiago's elusive statements. I had grown used to them by now. From the moment we met, there had been something about him I couldn't quite grasp. It wasn't just familiarity—it was the unsettling sense that he knew me long before we met.

"Why do people call you Caminante?" I asked.

Santiago smiled. "It's short for Caminante de la Cumbre."

Osvaldo looked up from his kitchen duties when he heard the name.

"It loosely translates as the Walker of the Peaks."

"Hmm, I guess that's fitting," I said.

I looked up at the night sky, only to see it was overcast again.

"You know something that's been bugging me?" I asked. "Since I got on this mountain, I have not seen the stars, not even once."

Santiago looked over. "Yes, it's a shame. They're so beautiful it's hard to describe. But that's the thing in the mountains, the weather—it can change in an instant, and then change right back again. You almost have to experience it to believe it."

The lantern must have been set to "high" because it lit up our entire camp and created a nice atmosphere for our final night.

"I need to talk to you about tomorrow," Santiago said, as he sat up in his snow chair. His voice suddenly became more serious.

"It will take about five hours in good weather to reach the summit, but there's no place to camp up there, so you have to make it to the top and get back down to High Camp on the same day. Just to be safe, you'll need to leave here around 2:30 a.m., which isn't too long from now."

"Wait, what do you mean, 'I'll have to leave'? Are you not coming?"

Santiago hesitated a moment before answering. "Neither of us are. You must make the final summit push alone."

"You can't be serious!" I exclaimed. "Who made that rule?"

"It's the way it is, Riley. You started this climb alone the moment you left your car that night in the desert, and you must finish it alone. It's your climb—it always has been."

"I can't even take Osvaldo with me?" I asked.

"No, but the way to the summit is clear. You ascend a narrow ridge all the way. There are a couple of exposed places, but you'll find fixed ropes there, and you know how to clip in and transfer your lines over the anchors. Near the top, there's one last section you'll have to scramble up, but you'll be fine."

Every time I thought I knew what lay ahead, the mountain seemed to throw me a curveball.

"I have to be honest. I don't like the sound of this. I don't want to climb alone."

225

High Camp

"You won't be," he said. "Trust the whispers of the mountain and you'll be fine. But you should sleep soon because tomorrow will be a long day for you."

I knew it wouldn't do any good to protest. Besides, I was fading fast. "Okay then, I guess I'll hit the hay. But I'm going to see you in the morning, right?" I asked.

"Of course. We'll make sure you have everything you need. Osvaldo will have your gear ready."

I handed my bowl back to Osvaldo and returned to my tent. I felt a mix of dread and relief. Dread, because I wasn't sure what lay ahead tomorrow. Relief, knowing this would soon be over. It had not been easy.

As I nestled into my sleeping bag, I pulled out my journal and opened it to the back page. So far the only words were:

I will honor my path.
I'm enough as I am.
I will live in a Beautiful State no matter what.

Just underneath, I wrote:

Keep climbing!

I realized I'd been collecting mantras and proclamations from my climb. But before I could give it any more thought, my eyelids fluttered and I drifted off to sleep.

Before I knew it, Santiago's voice called my name from outside the tent. "Riley, it's time."

As I sat up in my sleeping bag, I heard the familiar sounds of zippers opening and the crunching of snow as

Santiago and Osvaldo walked. The lights from headlamps moved through the dark, occasionally sweeping past my tent and briefly providing light.

I got up as quickly as I could, ignoring my body's protest. I put on my layers and headed out into the dark. It was the coldest morning yet—you could feel it in your eyes. I stumbled over to the lantern, and Osvaldo handed me my coffee. A moment later, he passed me a bowl of oatmeal.

The sky was still overcast, but at least it was calm—calm, except for inside of me. I felt a gnawing in the pit of my stomach. Santiago appeared out of the dark carrying my crampons, ice axe, and some other gear for clipping onto the fixed ropes.

"Let's get your crampons on now, and the rest you can carry in your pack until you need them. The idea is to take only what you need. Get up, and get back down. We don't linger on peaks this high."

As I gathered the last of my gear, I felt something else— sadness. While I looked forward to this being over, I also didn't want it to end. By my calculations this was our tenth day on the mountain. The opportunity to disappear and focus on recalibrating my life—on listening to my soul—was the opportunity of a lifetime. *How many people need this?* I thought.

"Okay, Riley," I said to myself. "Let's create the weather. I will live in a Beautiful State, no matter what," I said out loud.

I took a moment to reflect, to be grateful for the climb, for Santiago, and for everyone else who helped me. I thought about my identity, my mosaic of beliefs, and conjured up a few memories of times I'd faced other challenges by myself. I knew today would be tough, but I didn't have to be perfect. I just needed to keep climbing.

"I believe in me," I whispered. I was ready.

Osvaldo and Santiago walked me from my tent to the start of the ridge. While Osvaldo fiddled with the straps on my backpack, Santiago gave me final instructions.

"How are you feeling?" he asked.

"Nervous. I still wish you guys could come."

"Everything you need for this climb is already within you. It's been with you all along—you just needed the mountain to reveal it."

Santiago pointed up the mountain into the dark. "Just follow the ridge; it will take you all the way to the summit. It's narrow in places, like a knife's edge, so don't stray from the path because it's a long way down on either side."

"Okay," I said, letting out an anxious breath.

"Do you remember the first night you knocked on my door?" he asked.

"Yes, of course. I was so afraid."

"Do you remember the first words I said to you?" Santiago asked.

"Yes, you said I was 'slightly off course,' or something like that, and I was to wind up in your village."

"I wasn't talking about you physically that night. I was referring to your life," he said. "You were disconnected from who you were meant to be, living a life that was not worthy of you. I saw it right away. You've always been destined for more, Riley. And look at you now!"

Santiago's eyes grew misty as he smiled at me. "It's been an absolute pleasure to share this climb with you."

"I wish you were coming today," I said.

Santiago smiled gently. "Remember, you're never alone. I'll be with you in spirit every step of the way. Always. Now, let's get you to the top."

"¡Vamos!" yelled Osvaldo, giving me a big smile as he held two thumbs up.

"Thank you," I said. "Wish me luck, and I'll see you soon."

"Riley," Santiago said. "One more thing. When you reach the summit, look for the cairn. It's important."

I nodded, then tightened the straps on my pack and drove the sharp teeth of my crampons into the slope. With each step, my ice axe stabbed into the snow, steadying me like an old friend. My breath came in short, ragged bursts, but I forced myself to keep moving.

I was glad it was dark because it shielded me from seeing the dizzying drop on either side. It was windy, but Santiago had told me to expect that. I was feeling good, even though progress was slow. Up ahead in the dark, I saw a short ledge I would have to scale. I spotted the rope attached to the rock, and when I reached it, I pulled out my line and clipped in.

When I got to the anchor, my line tangled. *You idiot,* I thought. But as soon as the words formed, I caught them. They were so harsh.

"We're not going to speak like that," I said, and I kept moving.

The rest of the rock section was relatively easy, the most difficult part being the sound of my crampons as they scraped across frozen stone, like fingernails on a chalkboard. Once

229

High Camp

on top, another stretch of snow-packed ridge lay before me. I unclipped from the rope and pressed on. I must have climbed for two hours, pushing myself as fast as I could. I felt exposed up here. My lungs were burning, and so were my legs.

The ridge steepened, and the summit towered above me, closer now, but still seemingly unreachable. Without warning, the wind rose suddenly in a powerful gust, knocking me off balance as it threw snow in my face. I tried to shield my eyes with my gloves until it passed. But it didn't help.

The gusts became more intense, swirling about—first shoving me from the left, then from behind—as though the mountain were a schoolyard bully. What started as a calm morning was quickly turning angry.

What now? I thought. *You're not going to make this easy, are you?*

My pace faltered as the blowing snow stung my exposed cheeks like sharp needles. The windchill bit into my forehead, each gust like a hammer driving nails. I began to feel faint.

"Keep climbing," I said to myself as I refocused on the summit.

As more snow blew off the ridge, it felt like I was back in the whiteout. I stopped, worried I would stray off course and tumble down the ridge.

"Trust yourself, Riley," I whispered, and I continued taking small steps up the mountain.

I didn't even see the next section of rock—I just ran into it. Groping around, I found the fixed rope and clipped in. This section was slower. It was steeper, and the blowing snow made it almost impossible to see.

230

The Call to Climb

"You're not stopping me," I said as I leaned into the wind and cleared the obstacle, then continued up the ridge.

As if the mountain heard my challenge, the wind whipped into a roar. Another powerful gust pushed me off balance, and I stumbled sideways, forcing me to put one hand out to steady myself.

I was barely moving now, but I was moving. The pain in my face from the cold was unbearable. Even my teeth ached. I couldn't stand another minute. Falling to my knees, I bent over and tried to cover my face with my gloves.

Another gust hit me, pushing me to one side. I thrust the point of my ice axe into the snow beneath me and lay on top of it, as I'd been taught.

I'm going to blow off this ridge, I panicked. *How is this making sense? I'm almost at the top.*

I needed help. Maybe that was the test—to see if I had enough humility to ask for it.

I rolled over on my back as the wind drove ice crystals into my face.

"Santiago," I yelled, my voice drowned immediately by the wind.

"Santiago ... *help!* Osvaldo!" I yelled.

I strained to hear a reply, but there was none. Just the relentless howl of the wind. Then it hit me. "Help is not coming," I whispered.

Panic clawed at my mind, and for a moment I felt paralyzed. I wanted to curl up right there. I couldn't do this alone.

But then, somewhere deep inside me, a quieter voice spoke: *You're not helpless.*

231

High Camp

For a moment, the storm faded into the background. *I'm not helpless.* I had climbed this far. I had faced caves, avalanches, and exhaustion. I had battled my doubts and stared down dragons.

With the wind still raging around me, I took a deep breath and thought of Santiago's words the night before: *Everything you need for this climb is already within you.*

He was right.

"Keep climbing." I whispered to myself, then said it louder. "Keep climbing."

The words became a rhythm, matching the beat of my heart and the crunch of my crampons in the snow.

"Keep climbing, Riley."

Each step was an act of rebellion, a declaration that I would not give up, and that I *was* the captain of my soul. *There can't be many more steps to go,* I thought.

And then, in front of me, was the last obstacle—the small rock cliff before the summit. I clipped onto the rope and began pulling myself up the steep face. Each handhold felt firm, and my legs suddenly felt strong as each step thrust my body upward.

As I neared the top, the wind suddenly began to ease. And as I pulled myself up and onto the last rock, I collapsed face down to rest.

As if being chased away, the wind was reduced to a breeze while the snow that had been swirling around began to settle back on the ground. I looked up toward the summit and, in the dark, I could see the top of its pyramid, only a hundred meters ahead.

I stood up, my legs shaky, and a rush of emotion welled up inside me. *I'm going to make it.*

232

The Call to Climb

The clouds began to part, and for the first time, the mountain revealed its quiet majesty. Millions of stars, which had hidden themselves from me, now filled the sky, stretching endlessly above.

I stared, transfixed. I'd never seen so many in all of my life.

I continued to climb, and as the summit grew closer, a shooting star streaked across the sky. "Wow," I gasped as I looked up. A few steps later, there was another, and immediately one more, as it sped across the sky.

"Oh my goodness. The meteor shower! He was right," I said. *Of course he was.* I smiled.

As the sky on the horizon began to glow, I could see the cairn at the summit. It was so close—maybe twenty more steps.

I inhaled deeply, sucking as much oxygen as I could into my lungs.

Four more steps, Riley.
Three ... two ... one.

Chapter 25

Walker of the Peaks

Elevation 22,834 feet

As the first rays of sunlight broke over the horizon, I stood alone on the summit. The world opened up around me, endless peaks rising and falling like waves frozen in time. The sky burned with shades of orange and pink, as light spilled over the mountains, painting the snow on the summit.

Before me, the cairn stood, lonely and weathered, a testament to those who had come before. It felt ancient, like a guardian of something. I dropped to my knees, partly out of exhaustion but mostly out of respect. My breath came in shallow gasps. This wasn't just a mountain, it was something greater. This entire experience had been—spiritual.

As the sky grew lighter, I felt a deep sense of gratitude. For all the days I struggled, and even questioned what life was about, I suddenly felt at peace, as if a great question had been answered that I didn't know I was asking.

I looked down at the pile of black rocks in front of me, and something caught my eye—a flash of red hiding beneath the stones. I remembered Santiago had told me to look for the cairn. Could this be why?

I took off my gloves and began gently moving the stones away. As I did, a red velvet ribbon came into view. It looked delicate, like it didn't belong in this harsh place—and yet it felt perfectly right. It was tied neatly around a small wooden box about the size of a book. I pulled it from the cairn and set it on my lap. My fingers traced the soft ribbon, and for a moment, I just stared at it. What could be inside? I wondered. My chest tightened with a mixture of curiosity and excitement.

Slowly, I untied the ribbon, letting it fall into my lap. The box was smooth and worn, as though it had been waiting here for years. My hands moved on their own, lifting the lid with care, as though opening a treasure.

Inside, nestled against a cloth lining, was a mirror with a simple wooden frame. I hadn't looked into a mirror since I'd left Santiago's house the day before the climb. I carefully lifted it out and tilted it toward me, unsure of what I might see.

The face staring back was unrecognizable—scraped and dirty, with cracked lips and windburned cheeks. My hair stuck out in wild directions, a tangled mess under my hat. But it wasn't the disheveled appearance that caught my attention. It was the eyes.

They were fierce. Wild. Alive.

I stared into them, captivated. This was me, but not the me I had known. This was someone stronger, who had endured the storms, faced their dragons, and didn't stop climbing.

"What happened to you, Riley?" I whispered to my reflection.

"You look like you've been through hell," I answered myself. "But you've never looked better."

236

The Call to Climb

I hadn't noticed at first, but tucked into the edge of the mirror's frame was a small piece of paper. It felt like parchment, delicate and ancient. I carefully pulled it out and as I unfolded the note it revealed a message. Inside were neatly written words:

One day you will meet your Maker.
But today, you stare into the eyes of your Creator.
Create something Beautiful.

Tears welled up in my eyes as I read them again. *The eyes of your Creator.* I glanced back at my reflection, seeing not just the face of someone transformed, but the face of someone capable of shaping their own destiny.

A sudden gust of wind swept across the summit, startling me. I turned my head and felt it—a hand on my shoulder. I spun around, but there was no one there. Just the endless expanse of peaks and valleys below.

Maybe it was Santiago's spirit, the ancestors he often spoke of, or the mountain itself. I didn't know. But for the first time, I didn't need to.

"I promise," I whispered into the wind, "I will create something beautiful, and I will never leave my soul behind again."

I wanted to stay here all day, but I remembered Santiago's words about not lingering on the summit. I carefully placed the mirror back inside the box and put them in my pack. As I started my descent, I couldn't wait to show the guys what I found hidden in the cairn.

The descent was fast and smooth as I retraced my steps from this morning. After a couple of hours I saw the tents, tiny yellow dots against the snow. It looked quiet in High Camp, but as I got closer I noticed there were only two tents, not three. Maybe they had already begun packing up.

As I walked down the final section of the ridge, Osvaldo emerged from his tent and made his way toward me. He had a big smile on his face. I couldn't help but smile back. Without him and Santiago, I'd never have made it.

I stopped when I reached him, and he gave me a thumbs-up, his expression asking if I'd made it. I nodded with a smile, raising both thumbs in response. He gave me the biggest smile I'd ever seen on his face.

"Where's Santiago?" I asked as I looked past him at the two tents.

Osvaldo's smile faltered slightly, and he hesitated, rubbing the back of his neck as he searched for words.

"Escalando," he said, his voice quiet but deliberate.

I frowned, trying to piece it together because I didn't know that word. What concerned me most was his body language.

Osvaldo nodded emphatically, pointing again to the horizon.

"Otras montañas," he said. Then in broken English, "other mountains."

"He's gone?" I asked.

Osvaldo nodded.

Scrambling to figure out what was going on, the words suddenly hit me like a jolt. Flashes of Santiago's cryptic comments came rushing back to me from the day I arrived at his house until this morning at High Camp.

238

The Call to Climb

Chills ran down my spine. He wasn't just a guide. He was sent here to lead me up this mountain and back to myself. And now his work was done. Tears blurred my vision as I looked out toward the peaks.

Osvaldo nodded as if agreeing with my thoughts. He'd been through this before with others.

He'd been sent for me, I realized.

I took a deep breath as Osvaldo gently reached out his hand to take my ice axe.

"Vamos," Osvaldo said softly, snapping me back to the present.

"Right," I said. "We still have to descend to Camp Two."

I began processing everything I'd learned and the decisions I'd made.

I will honor my path.
I am enough as I am.
I will live in a beautiful state.
I will keep climbing.

"Because," I whispered to the wind. "I am the creator of my life."

Osvaldo gave me a thumbs-up again, his expression asking if I was ready.

"Yes," I said, a small smile spreading across my face.

"Vamos!" he said energetically.

"Vamos!" I echoed back.

As we started down, I looked out at the vast horizon. Endless peaks stretched before me, each one a challenge, a possibility—an invitation.

A smile spread across my face.

The mountains were calling. And I was born to climb.

Walker of the Peaks

Feeling Called to Climb? Visit:
www.iwillclimb.com
Or scan:

Acknowledgments

The idea for *The Call to Climb* first came to me twelve years ago. The story is a culmination of my own journey and of those I've worked with over the last three decades. Many people have contributed to the ideas and concepts in the book—some I know personally, while others have contributed by their own work and expertise. I want to take the opportunity to acknowledge them here.

First and foremost, I want to express my deepest gratitude to Dr. James Hollis. Dr. Hollis, a Jungian analyst and author of twenty books, profoundly influenced this project. His book *Finding Meaning in the Second Half of Life* found me during my own dark night of the soul and offered me a lifeline of understanding. His insights about the collision of selves, the restoration of personal autonomy, and the soul's summons to an appointment planted the seeds for Riley's journey up the mountain.

Dr. Hollis has been incredibly generous with his time, exchanging emails with me and graciously appearing on my podcast. His wisdom and kindness have left an indelible mark on both this book and my life. Many of Santiago's teachings, particularly in the early chapters, are inspired by Dr. Hollis's work. He was the one who told me, "When the path is right, the

241

energy is there." I highly recommend his work to anyone seeking deeper self-understanding.

I also wish to acknowledge other thought leaders whose work has shaped my thinking and contributed to this book. Michael Singer's *The Untethered Soul* inspired some of the ideas in the cave scene, where Santiago teaches Riley to observe their emotions and disconnect from them. Marisa Peer, a renowned therapist and creator of Rapid Transformational Therapy (RTT), introduced me to the concept that "You need to make the unfamiliar, familiar." This idea is echoed in Riley's transformative moments.

Michael Bolduc, a success coach and personal friend, introduced me to the concept of the Beautiful State, which he learned from Preethaji and Krishnaji. Their book *The Four Sacred Secrets: For Love and Prosperity, a Guide to Living in a Beautiful State* has been another invaluable resource.

The late Morty Lefkoe was the first to teach me how to identify limiting beliefs and change them.

In addition to these sources of inspiration, my faith in God has been a constant thread throughout my life. Like Riley's journey through avalanches and caves, my faith journey has had its ups and downs. Yet through it all, I've seen a divine thread weaving through my story, for which I am grateful.

I also want to thank the entire team at Wiley for believing in this project and working alongside me to bring it to life. A special thank you to Cheryl Segura, whose persistent follow-up and encouragement helped finally get this book out of base camp.

To my high school English teacher, Ms. Malner-Charest, who encouraged me to write when I didn't think I could. Thank you for your patience and belief.

To the many friends who have supported me over the years—your contributions to my journey are too numerous to name here. At times you've been my Santiago, offering wisdom and guidance, and at others you've been my Osvaldo, providing quiet support while I summoned the courage to take "one more step."

To my parents: My mother, who read to me every night as a child, instilled in me a love for books, while my father's stories of his adventures in the woods inspired my love of exploration. I was fortunate to grow up in a loving family with my siblings (Jeff, Heather, and Jenny) on a small cattle ranch in the foothills of the Rocky Mountains.

Lastly, to my rope team—my three not-so-little climbers, Amber, Braden, and Sydney. You have been the best part of my journey and the main reason I climb. I hope this book inspires you to believe in possibility and bring the most authentic version of yourself to this life, because who you are is the gift you bring to the world.

Thank you for reading *The Call to Climb*.

James R. Robbins

About the Author

James Robbins grew up on a small cattle ranch in the foothills of the Rocky Mountains, where he developed a deep appreciation for hard work, resilience, and the beauty of nature. Today he helps individuals and organizations reach their highest potential through transformative leadership strategies and personal growth.

James's first book, *Nine Minutes on Monday*, was named the number one business book of the year in 2012 by Canada's *Globe and Mail*. He has earned a reputation as a thought leader in leadership development and his presentations have inspired audiences around the globe.

Index

Acceptance, 99, 130–131
Accomplishments,
    87, 136, 154
Acquaintances, 174
Action, committing to, *see*
    Committing to act
Alignment with soul's intent:
    achieving, 235–237
    barrenness of life without,
       53–54, 57
    examined life for, 79–80
    forces in opposition to,
       21–24
    as goal, 82
    identity for, 100
    purpose and, 88
    pursuing (*see* Soul's path)
    signs of not being in, 4–5,
       20–25, 47, 92, 228
    worthy pursuit and,
       210–211

Ancestors, strength from,
    135–136
Anger:
    detachment from, 143
    at facing "dragons," 125
    forgiveness and letting go
       of, 176, 183, 196
    protection from, 35
    in Turbulent State, 167, 200
    and worthy pursuit, 208
Anxiety, 24, 69, 78–79, 112,
    120–124, 130, 144
Approval seeking, 21–22,
    65–66, 91–92,
    125, 132, 155
Aristotle, 64
Authentic life, ix, 21, 69, 80,
    83–88, 176, 210
Autonomy, 99
Autopilot, 73, 92, 101,
    143, 159

Awareness:
of emotions and beliefs,
141–142, 159
of programs and patterns,
68, 70, 72–73, 77, 94

Beautiful State, 167–169,
172, 173, 175,
182, 197–200, 227
Behavioral patterns, *see*
Patterns of behavior
Belief(s):
changing, 77–78, 112,
151, 153
emotions and, 148–149, 159
empowering vs. limiting,
110–111
in mosaic of identity,
109–111, 159
and programs, 63
in purpose-filled life, 27
reframing, 149–150
in soul, 30
and spiritual vision, 86
sustaining, 218, 219
in yourself, 228, 230–232
Betrayal, 176–178
Bodily reactions and
sensations, 73, 143

Boundaries, in relationships,
174–176
Busyness, 27

Capable, feeling, 99, 134
Career:
job loss, 34–35, 92, 211
purpose vs. activities of,
84–85
worthy pursuit and,
207, 210, 211
Change, 19
in beliefs, 77–78,
112, 151, 153
deciding to make, 9–10
fear of, 6, 8, 35–36
interrupting patterns
with, 57
in programs, 69–70,
77–78, 82,
98–99, 150
subconscious/internal
resistance to,
69, 78, 98–99
Childhood, 64, 109,
111, 148–149, 206
Climb:
to align life with soul's
intent (*see* Soul's path)

being called to (*see* Soul,
summons from)
finding a guide for,
17–20, 238–239
to honor appointment
with soul, 25–27
reluctance to undertake,
29–31
signals to begin, 20–25,
31–35
Comfort zone, leaving,
69, 141–142
Committing to act:
to create your own
destiny, 239
despite conflicting values, 6
to follow the soul's path,
14, 102, 145, 158, 229
Companions on your
journey, 174
Compassion, 137
Connection. *See also*
Relationship(s)
to God, 119, 135, 165–166
to nature, 119, 135,
165–166
and safety, 145–147
soul's desire for, 172–174,
200, 210, 221

Consistency, 218
Control, 69, 92, 99, 112,
143–144, 159
Conviction, 155
Courage, 91, 130, 154, 176,
220
Creator, *see* God
Crisis, 24, 47
Curiosity, 72

Decision making, 9–10, 35
Depression, 24, 141
Destiny, creating your own,
237–240
Detachment:
from emotions, 142–144,
146–148, 150, 159,
188–189
from fears, 146–147
from judgment, 72, 74–76,
142–143, 148
from pain, 216–217
Disappointment, 21,
52, 169, 172
Discomfort:
with conflict, 74
with emotions, 143
finding meaning of,
214–216

Discomfort (*Continued*)
on soul's path, 12,
42, 71, 81,
103, 141, 227
Discouraged, feeling, 80,
118, 209, 216
Doubt, 12, 40, 44,
111–112
Dragons, *see* Soul wounds
Dreams, as messages from
soul, 42–43

Ego:
alignment of job/career
with, 210
masks created by,
99–100, 129
meaning driven by,
110–111
overthrowing, 80
programs and patterns
associated with,
65, 92–92
soul's conflict with, 21–24,
41, 47, 65–66
validation seeking by,
134–135
Emotional triggers, 142, 151,
175, 177, 184, 188

Emotions:
beliefs underlying,
148–149, 159
detaching from, 142–144,
146–148, 150, 159,
188–189
energy and, 142–143,
167–169
preventing forgiveness,
192, 196
Empowering beliefs, 110
Energy. *See also* Beautiful
State; Turbulent State
emotions and, 142–143,
167–169
getting in touch with,
165–167
and inner life, 40, 166–167,
183, 200, 224, 227
from letting go, 192–193
to pursue purpose, 83–84
and spiritual vision, 86
for worthy pursuits,
209, 211
Enough, believing you are,
137, 157, 158, 164
Examined life, 68, 72–76,
79–80, 92, 94, 143
Expectations, others', 85, 88

Experiences:
  meaning of, 110–111,
    133, 149
  in mosaic of identity,
    109–110, 159
  painful, 64–65, 111,
    136–137, 177–179, 184
Exploration, 59–60

Failure:
  ego vs. soul's mindset
    on, 134–135
  fear of, 52, 125, 159, 216
  patterns of behavior
    leading to, 55–56
  protective programs
    and, 67
  reflecting on, 114, 118
Fairness, 190–191
Faith, 217–219
Fear(s), 11–12, 32
  of change, 6, 8, 35–36
  deep, 111–112, 125, 130
  detaching from, 146–147
  as drivers of emotion, 148
  examining, 152–153
  facing, 105, 111–112, 140
  of failure, 52, 125,
    159, 216

reclaiming life from, 144
of rejection, 110, 111,
  159, 205
as sanction from
  subconscious, 69
of soul wounds/dragons,
  130, 159
in Turbulent State, 167, 200
First step, taking, 36, 100
Forgiveness, 178–179,
  183–184, 189–196, 200
Freedom:
  after facing fears/soul's
    wounds, 127–128,
    131–132
  after forgiveness and, 184,
    189–190, 192, 196
  detachment from emotions
    for, 144, 147
Fundamental needs, 99, 111,
  136–137

Gifts, sharing your,
  132–133
Glacier, see Subconscious
Goals, 86, 113–114,
  132, 157
God:
  bargains with, 40

251

Index

God (*Continued*)
connection to, 119,
135, 165–166
fighting "dragons" with,
131, 133
forgiving, 193–194, 196
guidance sent by, 238–239
Gratitude, 97, 169, 235
Grief, 169
Grit, 154, 215–216, 218
Growth, 134–136, 215
Grudges, 176, 182, 200
Guilt, 51–52, 182, 194

Habits, building, 172, 218
Happiness, 168, 169,
172, 209
Heart, as prison, 177–179,
182, 184
Henley, William, 92
Hobbies, as worthy
pursuits, 208–209
Hope, 9, 12–13, 36, 219

Identity:
building new, 151–152
choosing your, 100,
149–150
control over, 112

in integrated life, 137
as mosaic, 109–110, 159
narratives and, 153
as source of strength,
99, 101
Inner child, 136–137, 155, 159
Inner circle (rope team),
58–59, 173–176, 199,
200, 219, 221, 238–239
Inner life, 40, 166–167, 174,
183, 200, 224, 227
Insecurities, 125. *See also*
Soul wounds
Instincts, ignoring, 5, 24
Integrated life, 136–137, 159
Intentional life, 85–86, 93,
142–143, 168, 172, 218
Internal resistance to change,
69, 78, 98–99
Iwillclimb.com, ix, 47, 94, 159,
200, 221, 240

Journal, recognizing patterns
in, 55–56
Judgment, detachment from,
72, 74–76, 142–143,
148

Kindness, 137, 154

Law of a Thousand
Steps, 218, 221
Letting go:
energy release from,
192–193
forgiveness for, 176–178,
182–184, 200
as soul's desire, 164–165,
173, 189
for subconscious, 78–79
Limiting beliefs, 110–111
Lost, feeling:
being unaligned with soul's
intent and, 3, 7–8, 17
on soul's path, 185, 188
as summons from soul,
20, 26, 27
Love, 99, 130–131, 169, 210

Mantras, 217
Marley, Bob, 198, 199
Masks, 99–100, 109, 129, 159
Meaning, 110–111, 133,
149, 205–206,
214–216, 219
Meditation, 114, 172, 197
Memories, 62, 192
Mindfulness, 72, 94
Mysticism, science and, 166

Narratives (stories):
about wealth and success,
67–68, 73–74, 77–78
with emotional charge,
77–78
exploring, in examined life,
74–76
identity and, 153
in mosaic of identity,
109–110
and patterns of behavior,
73–74
and protective programs,
63–64, 66
reclaiming your, 100, 150
rewriting, 77–78, 94
Nature, connection to, 119,
135, 165–166
Negativity, 118
"No," saying, 73–76

One more step, taking, 52,
213–215. See also
Perseverance
One with divine hands,
see God
Optimism, 118
Overwhelmed, feeling,
134, 216

253

Index

Pain:
detachment from, 216–217
reframing meaning of,
214–216, 219
worthy pursuit and,
207–208
Painful experiences:
avoiding, 136–137
heart as prison after,
177–179, 184
programs formed by, 64–65
wounds to soul
related to, 111
Parents, 67–68, 73–74,
77–78, 195
Passion, 24, 84, 207
Patterns of behavior:
awareness of, 68, 72–73, 94
breaking, to build new
identity, 151–152
ego and, 92–93
in examined life, 72–73
payoff for repeating, 74–76
predicting future behavior
from, 56–57
programs as drivers of, 63,
68–70, 94
recognizing, 54–56, 68
Peace, 88, 125, 193, 197, 205

Perfectionism, 134, 155,
199, 227
Perseverance, 120–123, 127,
213–215, 217, 219,
221, 226–228, 230–233
Powerlessness, 134, 191
Protective programs:
awareness of, 70, 72–73, 94
changing, 69–70,
77–78, 82, 98–99, 150
as drivers of patterns,
63, 68–70, 94
energetic state dictated
by, 168
forgiving parents for, 195
and identity, 101, 109
reactions in body to, 73
root cause of, 74–76
subconscious as
source of, 63–66
surface clues of, 72–73
Purpose, 21
authentic life as,
83–85, 88
as expression of soul,
87, 88
finding, 82–83, 86–87,
94, 205
of pain, 216–217

254

Index

reconnecting to, 217

tasks or activities vs., 82–85

Purpose-filled life, ix, 27, 200

Quitting, 44–45, 51–52, 98,
184, 190, 213–214

Reality, truth vs., 131

Reciprocity, 175–176

Reconciliation, 183–184

Reflection, see Self-reflection

Rejection, 65, 67–68, 99, 110,
111, 159, 205

Relationship(s):
gratitude for, 97
guidance from, 141,
238–239
safety from, 58–59
soul's desire for, 172–174
strength from, 133–134,
175–176, 221
threats to, 67–68, 78
types of, 174–175
with yourself, 115

Relaxation, 219–220

Resentment, 191

Resilience, 118, 215–216,
218, 221

Respect, 17, 91–92

Responsibility, taking, 137

Rope team, see Inner circle

Science, mysticism and, 166

Security, 39–40

Self-criticism, 118, 124–125,
129, 144, 153–156,
159, 229

Self-praise, 154, 155, 159

Self-reflection:
on Beautiful State, 171–172
being overwhelmed by, 71
on conflicting values, 11–12
for examined life, 71, 74, 77
on failure, 114, 118
to find spiritual vision, 88
to gauge progress, 29, 66,
71, 156–157, 220,
227, 236–237
for gratitude, 227
on identity, 99
on impact of soul's journey,
236–237
on inner life and energy,
40, 166–167
on messages from
subconscious, 66, 74, 77
on self-worth,
156–157, 220

255

Index

Self-reflection (*Continued*)
on soul wounds/fears,
124–125, 144–145
and summons from
soul, 23, 46
Self-sabotage, 67, 73–74
Self-worth, 130–131
Service, 207
Shame, 5, 111, 130, 144,
157, 182, 194
Significance, of pursuit, 208
Silence, 11, 115
Soul:
alignment with intent of
(*see* Alignment with
soul's intent)
Beautiful State and, 173
belief in, 30
conversation with, 46
death of, 44–45
defined, 21, 41
desire of, for connection/
relationships, 172–174,
200, 210, 221
dreams as messages
from, 42–43
ego's conflict with,
21–24, 41, 47,
65–66, 68–69

honoring appointments
with, 25–27
layers of, 209
letting go as desire of,
164–165, 173, 189
meaning of experiences
driven by, 110–111,
133, 149
not abandoning, 89–90,
93, 109
purpose as expression
of, 87, 88
pursuit of growth by,
134, 135
subconscious vs.,
65–66, 68–69
summons from, 8,
22–25, 47
uprising of, 80
worth of, 88
Soul's path:
attempting to follow
someone else's, 90–91
challenges/difficulties
along, 79, 90, 92, 98,
102–104, 108–109,
121–122, 203–204,
223, 230–231
changing nature of, 62

danger along, 38–40,
139–141
deciding to pursue,
35–36, 47
discomfort on, 12, 42, 71,
81, 103, 141, 227
energy to pursue, 209, 211
explaining, to others,
223–224
finding, around obstacles,
103–104, 107–108, 115
guidance on, 17–20,
238–239
honoring your, 91–92,
163, 226
ongoing journey of, 90–91
overriding programs
to follow, 65
perseverance on,
120–123, 127
rewards for following,
233, 236–237
sanctions from subcon-
scious on, 69
signs you are following,
151–152, 156
as solo journey, 225–226,
229, 235
staying on, 228

summons to undertake, 8,
22–25, 47
worthiness and, 132
Soul wounds (dragons), 111
awareness to tame,
141–142
detachment to tame, 144
as drivers of emotion, 148
facing, 122–125,
127–129, 159
fighting, 129–130, 135
forgiveness and, 191
freedom after taming,
131–132
Spiritual vision, 85–88, 94,
152, 153, 176
Strength:
ancestors as source of,
135–136
challenges to build,
219–220
identity as source of,
99, 101
from inner circle/rope
team, 219, 221
from perseverance,
214–215, 217
Strong, need to feel, 99, 134
Stuck, feeling, 121–123, 171

257

Index

Subconscious (glacier):
awareness of, 70
desires of soul vs.,
65–66, 68–69
examining, 61, 62, 66
exploring narratives from,
74–76
giving into emotions
and, 143
and honoring your path, 92
letting go by, 78–79
protective programs from,
63–65
resistance to change from,
69, 78
Suffering, 168, 184,
190–191, 217
Survival threats, 65

Thoughts:
being alone with, 112–115
energy contained in, 166
learning to sit with, 118
"Three Little Birds" (song),
198, 199
Transactional relationships,
174–175
Trust, 13–15, 18
Truth, 100, 125, 130, 131, 159
Turbulent State, 167–169,
172, 176

Unfamiliar, embracing the,
151–152, 217–218
Uniqueness, 132–133

Validation, 131–132, 134–135
Value, adding, 99, 132–134
Values:
being swayed by others', 25
conflicts involving, 3–7,
11–12, 20–21, 207–208
getting clear on, 86
Vamos, see Committing to act
Vision, spiritual, *see*
Spiritual vision

Wealth, narratives about,
67–68, 73–74, 77–78
Worry, in Turbulent
State, 167, 200
Worth, 88
"dragons" related to, 65
intrinsic, 131–132, 158, 159
praise and recognition of,
155–157
self-worth, 130–131
triggering of soul wounds
around, 191
Worthy pursuit, 85,
205–208, 221